A-Z CAMBRIDGE

D1263847

CONTENTS

Key to Map Pages	Back Cover
Large Scale Pages	2-3
Map Pages	4-33
Index to Streets, Towns, Villages, Hospitals, and Selected Places of Interest	34-47
Index to Colleges	48

REFERENCE

Motorway	M11		Cycle Route	🚲 .....
A Road	A14		Church or Chapel	†
B Road	B1049		Fire Station	■
Dual Carriageway			Hospital	Ⓗ
One Way Street — Traffic flow on A Roads is indicated by a heavy line on the drivers left	→		House Numbers — A & B Roads Only	83 96
Large Scale Pages Only	→		Information Centre	🄸
Restricted Access			National Grid Reference	⁵45
Pedestrianized Road			Police Station	▲
Track			Post Office	★
Footpath			Toilet — With facilities for the Disabled	▽ ♿
Residential Walkway			Educational Establishment	
Railway — Level Crossing — Station			Hospital or Hospice	
Built Up Area	MILL ST.		Industrial Building	
Local Authority Boundary	· — · —		Leisure or Recreational Facility	
Postcode Boundary			Cambridge University, College/Hall	
Map Continuation	20 Large Scale City Centre 2		Place of Interest	
			Public Building	
Car Park selected	P		Shopping Centre or Market	
Park & Ride	P+🚌		Other Selected Buildings	

Scale 1:16,896

0 — ¼ — ½ Mile
0 — 250 — 500 — 750 Metres

3 ¾" (9.53 cm) to 1 mile
5.92cm to 1km

Copyright of Geographers' A-Z Map Co. Ltd.

Head Office:
Fairfield Road, Borough Green, Sevenoaks, Kent TN15 8PP
Telephone 01732 781000 (Enquiries & Trade Sales)
01732 783422 (Retail Sales)

www.a-zmaps.co.uk

Copyright © Geographers' A-Z Map Co. Ltd.

 Ordnance Survey This product includes mapping data licensed from Ordnance Survey® with the permission of the Controller of Her Majesty's Stationery Office.

© Crown Copyright 2002. All rights reserved. License Number 100017302

Edition 3 2002, Edition 3b 2005 (Part Revision)

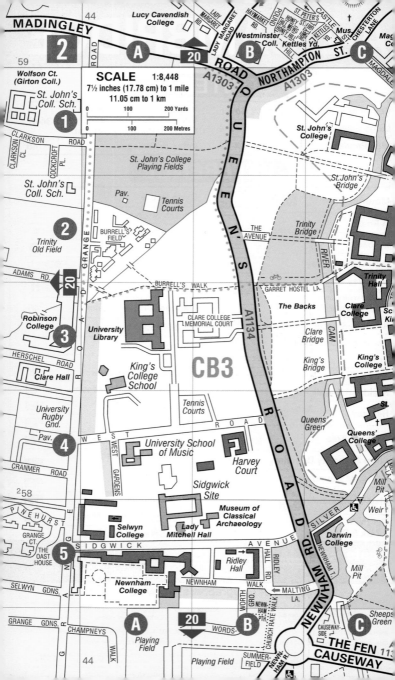

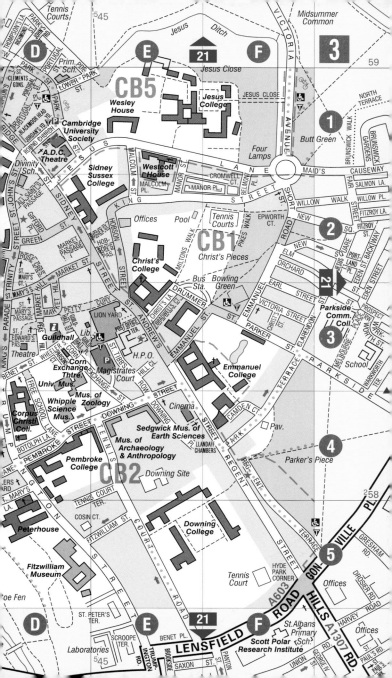

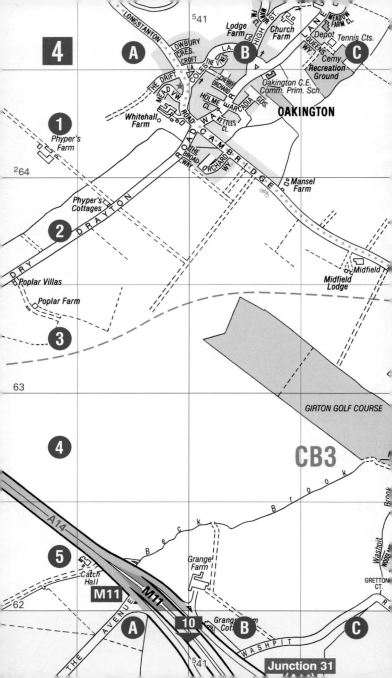

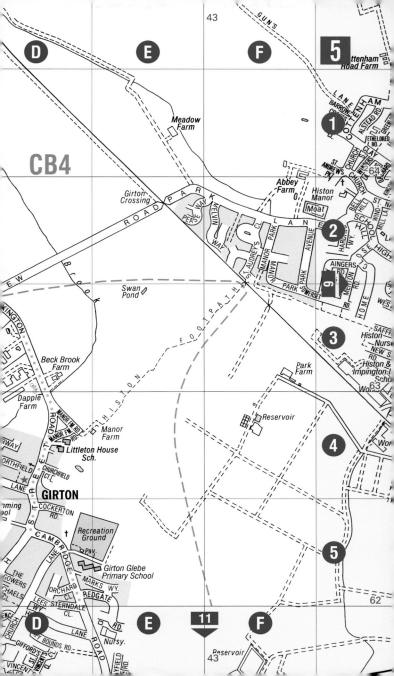

D   **E**   **F**   **5**   ttenham Road Farm

43   GUN'S

CB4

1

Meadow Farm

Abbey Farm

Histon Manor

St Andrews Pav.

264

Moat

Girton Crossing

ROAD

PARK

PEAS WAY

MELVIN WAY

ST AUDREY'S CL

MANOR PARK

PARK AVENUE

SOMERSET

2

AINGERS RD.

MELTON RD.

HOME

WEST

9

BROOK

EW

Swan Pond

FOOTPATH

HISTON

PARK RD.

3

Histon Nurs.

NEW S.

Histon & Impington Scho

63

Beck Brook Farm

Dapple Farm

ROAD

MANOR FM. RD.

Manor Farm

Littleton House Sch.

Park Farm

Reservoir

Wor

4

Wo

ORTHFIELD

CHURCHFIELD CT.

LANE

GIRTON

COCKERTON RD.

STREET

CAMBRIDGE

ming ol

GOWERS

MICHAELS

THE

ORCHARD CL.

LEES CL.

STERNDALE CL.

WY.

Recreation Ground

Pav.

Girton Glebe Primary School

MARKS WY.

REDGATE

5

62

GIFFORD'S

VINCENT'S

LANE ROAD

BOUNDS RD.

FIELD RD.

Nursy.

D   **E**   **11**   **F**

43   Reservoir

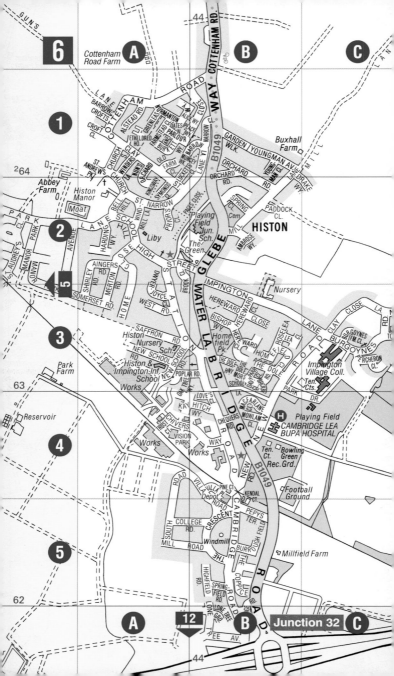

D **E** 46 **F** **7** Pur Fa...

Oldfield Farm

1

Bedlam Farm

2 64

Manor Farm

2

OST ANDREWS WY

North View

The Almonds

B R O A D

M E R E

8

Sun Close Farm

ST GEORG...

WY

Farm Depot

New Close Farm

CB4

Mere Way Poultry Farm

W A Y

BUTT

3

...PINGTON

LANE

Recycling Centre

63

M E R E

4

5

A14

62

BLACKWELL CARAVAN SITE

D KING'S HEDGES **E** RD. **13** **F**

Cambridge Regional Coll.

KING'S HEDGE

K I N G ' S

ROAD 46

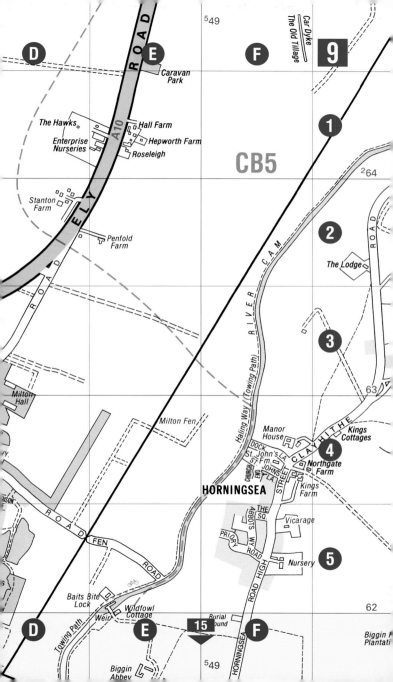

D   **E**   **F**   **9**

⁵49

Car Dyke
The Old Tillage

Caravan
Park

ROAD

1

The Hawks

Hall Farm

Enterprise
Nurseries

Hepworth Farm

A10

Roseleigh

CB5

²64

Stanton
Farm

ELY

2

ROAD

The Lodge

Penfold
Farm

ROAD

R I V E R   C A M

3

63

Milton
Hall

Milton Fen

(Towing Path)

Haling Way

4

CLAYHITHE

Manor
House

Kings
Cottages

DOCK
St. John's LA.
ST. JOHNS FM.
St. JOHNS LA.

Northgate
Farm

CHURCH END

STREET

HORNINGSEA

Kings
Farm

ROAD

FEN

THE
SQ.

Vicarage

ABBEY
CLOSE

PRIORY

ROAD

ROAD

5

Nursery

ROAD HIGH

62

Baits Bite
Lock

Wildfowl
Cottage

Weir

Towing Path

E

Burial
Ground

15

HORNINGSEA

F

D

⁵49

Biggin
Abbey

Biggin
Plantati

10

62

Catch Hall

THE AVENUE

B

5 41

Grange Farm
4

Grange Farm
Cottages

WASHPIT

A **B** **C**

GRETTON
CT.

Washpit
Wind...

R

1

M11

Junction
(A14

M11 MOTORWAY

2

Bulls
Close

61

Animal
Research
Station

Wes...

3

A428

CB3

**Junction 14
(M11)**

Sub...

Ladybush
Close

4

Wrangling
Corner

² 60

CAMBRIDGE

5

American
Military
Cemetery **P**

Moor Barn
Farm

Madingley
Wood

Madingley
Hill Mill Farm
Windmill

ROAD

ST. NEOTS

A **18** **B** ROAD M **A** **C** D

A1303

ROAD

Blue
Gates

Coton
Court

Sinoia
5 41

The
Bungalow

Rectory Far

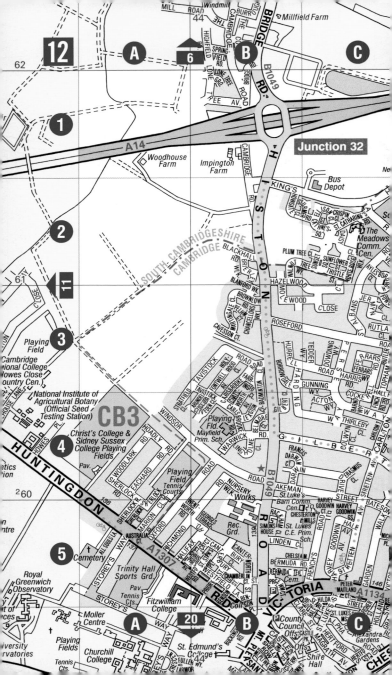

16

ROAD HIGH

Nursery

62

⁵50

(A)

(B)

(C)

Black

Biggin Pin
Plantation

Ditch

Th

1

DROVEWAY

LOW   FEN   Snout
                        Corner

LOW

FEN

2

DROVEWAY

Black

61

◄ **15**

CB5

3

DROVEWAY

Lo
No

Chapman's
Plantation

Ditch

Honey Hill

Upper
Norris

4

A14

FEN

²60 Ditch
Bridge

HIGH

LOW

Quy
Water

5

DITCH

Black
House

ROAD

CB1

Greenhouse
Farm

(A)

24

Quy Water
Farm

(B)

A1303

(C)

Longfield
Farm

N—E—W—M—A—R—K—E—T

⁵50

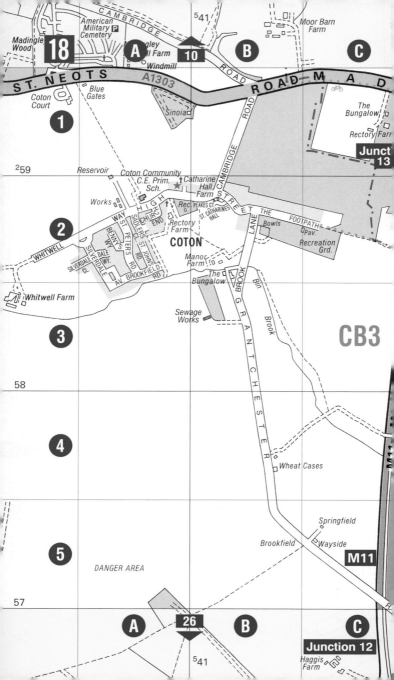

CAMBRIDGE

Madingle Wood

American Military Cemetery P

18

ngley ll Farm

Windmill

A

10

B

Moor Barn Farm

C

ST. NEOTS A1303

ROAD

ROAD

M A D

Coton Court

Blue Gates

1

Sinoiac

²59

Reservoir

Works

Coton Community C.E. Prim. Sch.

† Catharine Hall Farm

HIGH

WAY

CHURCH END

SADLERS

Rec.

PEAKES CT.

ST. CATHARINES HALL

Rectory Farm

COTON

2

ST. PETER'S RD.

BENNY'S

ST. JOHN'S RD.

WHITWELL

SILVERDALE

DALE WY.

SILVERDALE CL.

BROOKFIELD RD.

AV.

Manor Farm

The Bungalow

3

Whitwell Farm

Sewage Works

CAMBRIDGE

STREET

THE

Bowls

FOOTPATH

Pav.

Recreation Grd.

BROOK

LANE

Bin

Brook

GRANTCHESTER

ROAD

The Bungalow

Rectory Farm

Junct 13

CB3

58

4

Wheat Cases

57

5

DANGER AREA

Springfield

Brookfield

Wayside

M11

A

26

B

C

⁵41

Junction 12

Haggis Farm

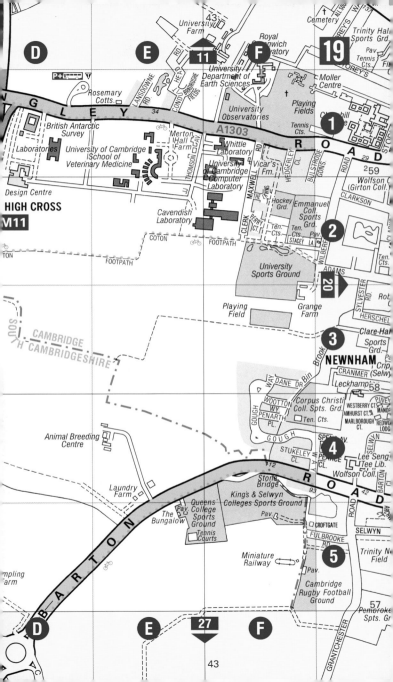

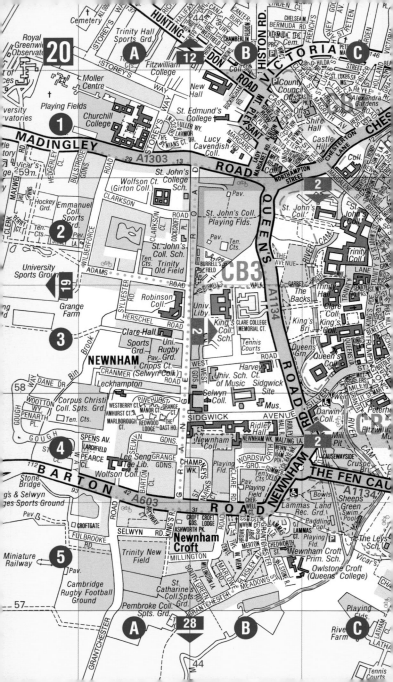

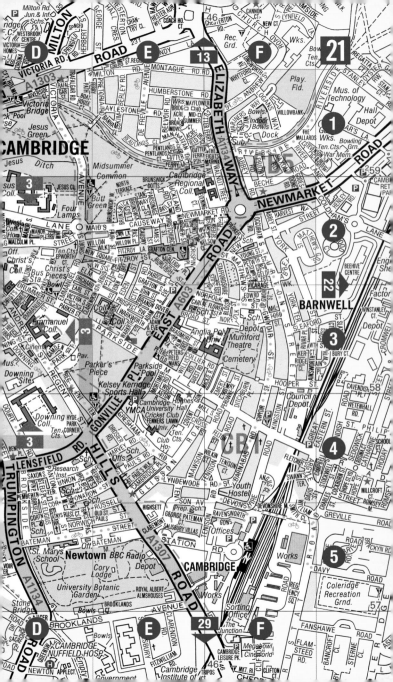

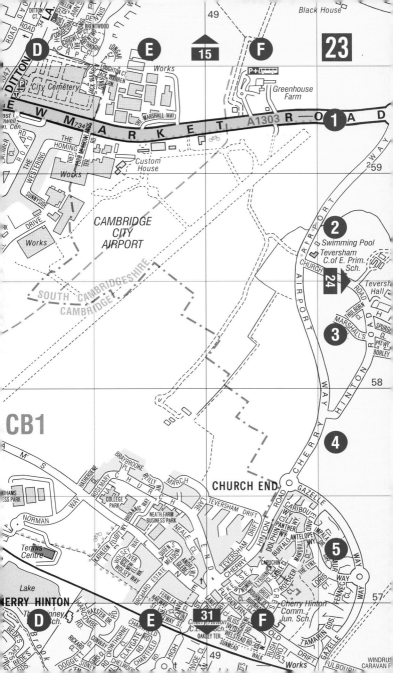

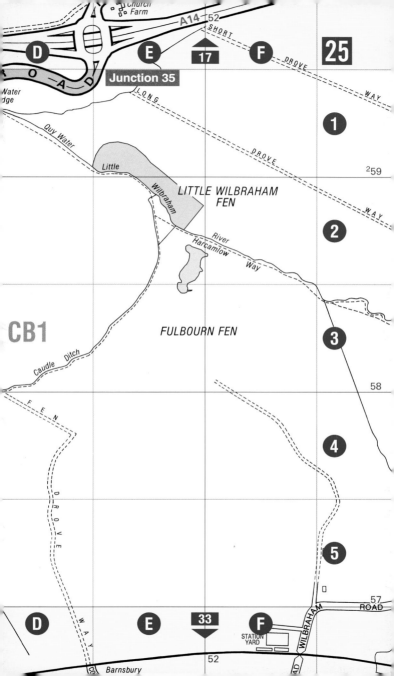

Church
Farm

A14 52

SHORT

D

E

F

17

DROVE

Junction 35

WAY

Water
dge

LONG

1

Quy Water

DROVE

Little

²59

Wilbraham

LITTLE WILBRAHAM
FEN

River

2

Harcamlow

Way

CB1

FULBOURN FEN

3

Caudle Ditch

58

F
E
N

4

D
R
O
V
E

5

57
ROAD

D

E

33

F

WILBRAHAM

WAY

STATION
YARD

52

Barnsbury

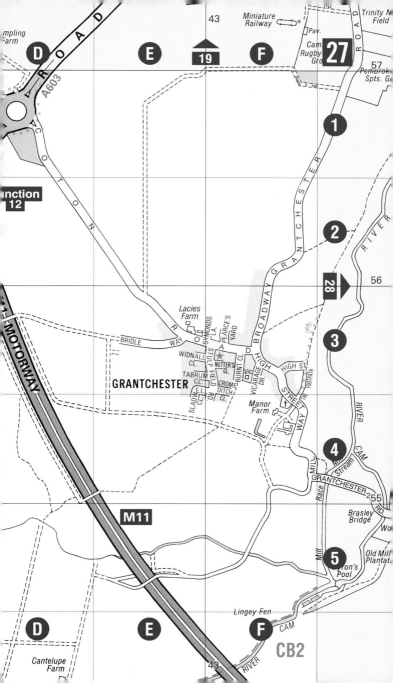

D **E** **19** **F** **27**

ROAD

A603

COTON

Junction **12**

Miniature Railway

Trinity N Field

Pav.

Cam Rugby Gro

Pembrok Spts. G

57

1

2

GRANTCHESTER ROAD

BROADWAY

RIVER

28 56

3

Lacies Farm

BRIDLE WAY

ROAD

SYMONDS LA.

PEARCE'S YARD

WIDNALL CL.

TABRUM CL.

SLADWEL CL.

FIELD CL.

NUTTER'S CL.

CROMER DITCH CL.

BURNT CL.

VICARAGE DR.

HIGH ST.

HIGH STREET

FOOTPATH

GRANTCHESTER

Manor Farm

MILL WAY

RIVER CAM

4

Stream

GRANTCHESTER RD.

255

Race

Brasley Bridge

Wo

M11

MILL

Old Mill Plantat.

5

...ton's Pool

MOTORWAY

Lingey Fen

F CAM

CB2

D **E**

Cantelupe Farm

43 RIVER

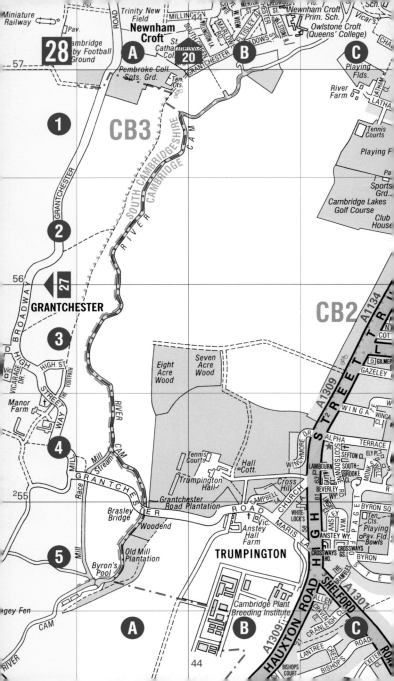

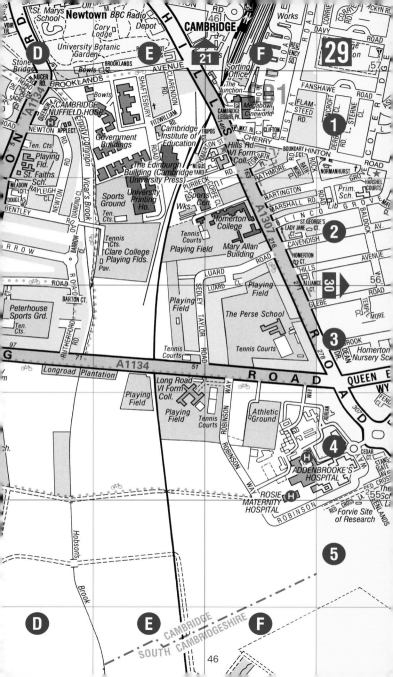

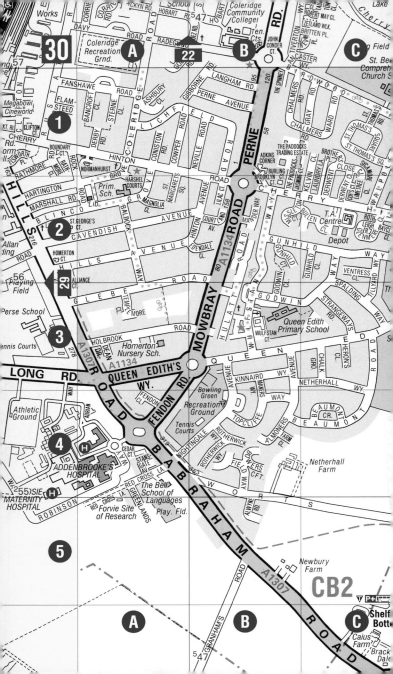

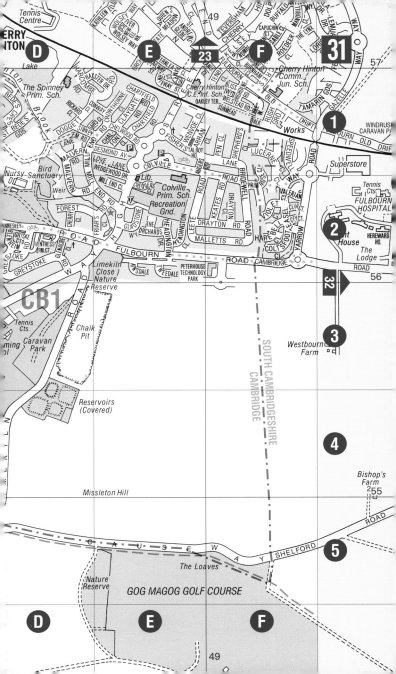

CB1

GOG MAGOG GOLF COURSE

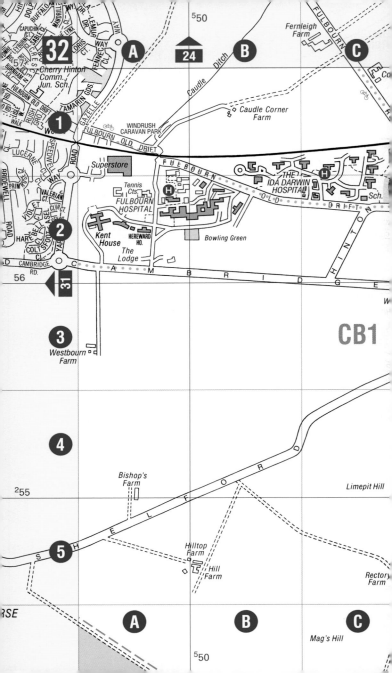

A   ▲ 24   **B**   **C**

Fernleigh Farm

Cherry Hinton Comm. Jun. Sch.

Caudle Ditch

1

Caudle Corner Farm

WINDRUSH CARAVAN PARK

FULBOURN OLD DRIFT

Superstore

FULBOURN

LUCERNE

RIDGEWELL

Tennis Cts

FULBOURN HOSPITAL

THE IDA DARWIN HOSPITAL

Sch.

H

H

OLD

DRIFT

2

Kent House

HEREWARD HO.

Bowling Green

FULBOURN

HINTON

The Lodge

CAMBRIDGE RD.

56

◄ **31**

C   A   M   B   R   I   D   G   E

3

Westbourn Farm

CB1

4

Bishop's Farm

²55

Limepit Hill

FORD

5

SHELFORD

Hilltop Farm

Hill Farm

Rectory Farm

RSE

A   **B**   **C**

Mag's Hill

⁵50

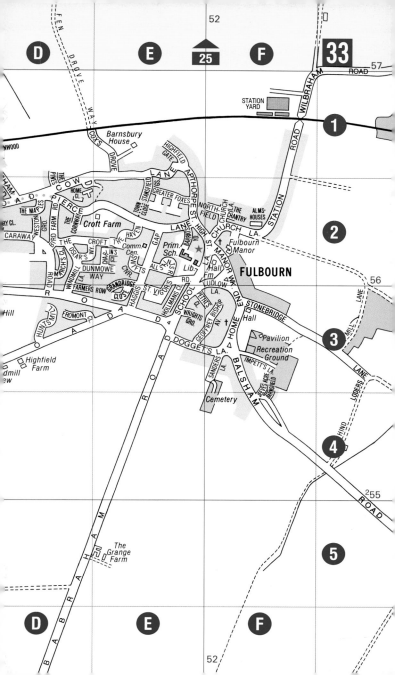

INDEX

Including Streets, Places & Areas, Hospitals & Hospices, Industrial Estates,
Selected Flats & Walkways and Selected Places of Interest.

HOW TO USE THIS INDEX

1. Each street name is followed by its Posttown or Postal Locality and then by its map reference;
   e.g. Abbey Rd. *Cam* . . . .1F **21** is in the Cambridge Posttown and is to be found in square 1F on page **21**.
   The page number being shown in bold type.

2. A strict alphabetical order is followed in which Av., Rd., St., etc. (though abbreviated) are read in full and as part
   of the street name; e.g. Barrowcrofts appears after Barrow Clo. but before Barrow Rd.

3. Streets and a selection of flats and walkways too small to be shown on the maps, appear in the index in
   Italics with the thoroughfare to which it is connected shown in brackets;
   e.g. *Alan Pervical Ct. Ches* . . . .5F **13** (off High St.)

4. Places and areas are shown in the index in **blue type** and the map reference is to the actual map square in
   which the town centre or area is located and not to the place name shown on the map;
   e.g. **Cambridge** 3C **20** (3D **3**)

5. An example of a selected place of interest is Cambridge & County Folk Mus. 1C **2**

6. An example of a hospital or hospice is ADDENBROOKE'S HOSPITAL 4A **30**

7. Map references shown in brackets; e.g. Adams Rd. Cam . . . .2A **20** (2A **2**) refer to entries that also appear
   on the large scale pages **2** & **3**.

GENERAL ABBREVIATIONS

All : Alley	La : Lane
App : Approach	Lit : Little
Arc : Arcade	Lwr : Lower
Av : Avenue	Mc : Mac
Bk : Back	Mnr : Manor
Boulevd : Boulevard	Mans : Mansions
Bri : Bridge	Mkt : Market
B'way : Broadway	Mdw : Meadow
Bldgs : Buildings	M : Mews
Bus : Business	Mt : Mount
Cvn : Caravan	Mus : Museum
Cen : Centre	N : North
Chu : Church	Pal : Palace
Chyd : Churchyard	Pde : Parade
Circ : Circle	Pk : Park
Cir : Circus	Pas : Passage
Clo : Close	Pl : Place
Comn : Common	Quad : Quadrant
Cotts : Cottages	Res : Residential
Ct : Court	Ri : Rise
Cres : Crescent	Rd : Road
Cft : Croft	Shop : Shopping
Dri : Drive	S : South
E : East	Sq : Square
Embkmt : Embankment	Sta : Station
Est : Estate	St : Street
Fld : Field	Ter : Terrace
Gdns : Gardens	Trad : Trading
Gth : Garth	Up : Upper
Ga : Gate	Va : Vale
Gt : Great	Vw : View
Grn : Green	Vs : Villas
Gro : Grove	Vis : Visitors
Ho : House	Wlk : Walk
Ind : Industrial	W : West
Info : Information	Yd : Yard
Junct : Junction	

POSTTOWN AND POSTAL LOCALITY ABBREVIATIONS

Bart : Barton	*Cot* : Coton
Cam : Cambridge	*Ful* : Fulbourn
Cax : Caxton	*Gir* : Girton
Ches : Chesterton	*Gran* : Grantchester

Posttown and Postal Locality Abbreviations

Has : Haslingfield
His : Histon
Horn : Horningsea
Imp : Impington
Land : Landbeach
Lin : Linton

Lode : Lode
Mil : Milton
Oak : Oakington
Stow : Stow-cum-Quy
Tev : Teversham
W Wick : West Wickham

A

Abbey Pool. 1B 22
Abbey Rd. *Cam* 1F 21
Abbey St. *Cam* 2F 21
Abbey Wlk. *Cam* .2F 21
Abbots Clo. *Cam* .2D 13
Abbots Way. *Horn* .5F 9
Abercorn Pl. *Cam* .1D 13
Acrefield Dri. *Cam* 1E 21
Acton Way. *Cam* .4C 12
Adam & Eve Ct. *Cam* 3E 21
Adam & Eve St. *Cam* 3E 21
Adams Rd. *Cam* 2A 20 (2A 2)
ADDENBROOKE'S HOSPITAL. 4A 30
Adkins Corner. *Cam* 1B 30
Adrian Way. *Cam* .4A 30
Aingers Rd. *His* 2A 6
Ainsdale. *Cam* 2E 31
Ainsworth Ct. *Cam* 3F 21
Ainsworth Pl. *Cam* 3A 22
Ainsworth St. *Cam* 3F 21
Airport Way. *Tev* 2F 23
Akeman St. *Cam* .4B 12
Akeman St. *Land* 1A 8
Alan Percival Ct. Ches 5F 13
(off High St.)
Albemarle Way. *Cam* 2D 13
Albert Rd. *Stow* 3F 17
Albert St. *Cam* 1D 21
Albion Row. *Cam* .1B 20
Albion Yd. Cam 1B 20
(off Albion Row)
Alder Ct. *Cam* 5F 13
Alec Rolph Clo. *Ful* 2C 32
Alex Wood Rd. *Cam* 3D 13
Alice Way. *His* 1A 6
Allen Ct. *Cam* 5C 28
Allens Clo. *Bart* 3A 26
Alliance Ct. *Cam* .2F 29
Allington Clo. *His* 1A 6
All Saint's Pas. *Cam* 2C 20 (2D 3)
All Saints Rd. *Ful* .2E 33
All Souls La. *Cam* .5A 12
Almoners Av. *Cam* 4B 30
Almshouses. *Ful* 2F 33
Alpha Rd. *Cam* 1C 20
Alpha Ter. *Cam* 4C 28
Alstead Rd. *His* 1A 6
Alwyne Rd. *Cam* .5B 30
Amblecote. Cam 3E 21
(off East Rd.)
Ambrose Way. *Imp* .2B 6
Amhurst Ct. *Cam* .4A 20
Amwell Rd. *Cam* .1E 13
Ancaster Way. *Cam* 5B 22
Anglers Way. *Cam* 4B 14
Angus Clo. *Cam* 4F 21
Annesley. *Cam* 2D 31
Ann's Rd. *Cam* 5D 15
Anstey Way. *Cam* .5C 28
Antelope Way. *Cam* 5F 23
Apollo Way. *Cam* .1D 13
Applecourt. *Cam* .1D 29
Apthorpe St. *Ful* 2E 33
Apthorpe Way. *Cam* 2F 13
Aragon Clo. *Cam* .2D 13
Arbury Ct. *Cam* 3D 13

Arbury Rd. *Cam* 2C 12
Arcadia Gdns. *Oak* .1B 4
Archway Ct. *Cam* .5A 20
Arden Rd. *Cam* 1E 13
Argyle St. *Cam* 4F 21
Armitage Way. *Cam* 1E 13
Arran Clo. *Cam* 1E 31
Arthur St. *Cam* 5C 12
Arundel Rd. *Cam* .4B 12
Ascham Rd. *Cam* .5D 13
Ashbury Clo. *Cam* 1A 30
Ashcroft Ct. *Cam* .2D 13
Ashfield Rd. *Cam* .4A 14
Ashley Ct. *Cam* 3F 21
Ashvale. *Cam* 2D 13
Ashworth Pk. *Cam* 5A 20
Atherton Rd. *Cam* .5E 13
Atkins Clo. *Cam* 2F 13
Auckland Rd. *Cam* 2E 21
Augers Rd. *Cam* 1E 31
Augustus Clo. *Cam* 1D 13
Australia Ct. *Cam* .5A 12
Avenue, The. *Cam* 2B 20 (2B 2)
Avenue, The. *Gir* 2A 10
Aylesborough Clo. *Cam* 2C 12
Aylestone Rd. *Cam* 1E 21

B

Babraham Rd. *Cam* 4A 30
Babraham Rd. *Ful* .5D 33
Badminton Clo. *Cam* 4B 12
Bagot Pl. *Cam* 1E 13
Bailey M. *Cam* 2E 21
Bakery Clo. *Fen D* .4D 15
Baldock Way. *Cam* 2A 30
Ballard Clo. *Mil* 3C 8
Balsham Rd. *Ful* 3F 33
Bancroft Clo. *Cam* 1A 30
Bandon Rd. *Gir* 3E 11
Banff Clo. *Cam* 2D 13
Banhams Clo. *Cam* 1E 21
Barnabus Ct. *Mil* 5B 8
Barnard Way. *Cam* 4C 12
Barnes Clo. *Cam* .2C 22
Barnsfield. *Ful* 4F 33
Barnwell. 3F 21
Barnwell Bus. Pk. *Cam* 2D 23
Barnwell Dri. *Cam* .2D 23
Barnwell Rd. *Cam* .3C 22
Barrats Yd. *Ful* 2E 33
Barrow Rd. *Cam* 2D 29
Barrowcrofts. *His* 1A 6
Barrow Rd. *Cam* 2D 29
Barton. 3A 26
Barton Clo. *Cam* 4A 20
Barton Rd. *Bart* 2C 26
Barton Rd. *Has* 5A 26
Bassett Clo. *Cam* .1E 13
Bateman M. *Cam* .5E 21
Bateman St. *Cam* .5D 21
Bateson Rd. *Cam* .5C 12
Baycliffe Clo. *Cam* 2C 30
Bayford Pl. *Cam* 1E 13
Beaconsfield Ter. *Cam* 5C 12
Beadles Trad. Est. *Cam* 5B 14
Beales Way. *Cam* .2F 13
Beaufort Pl. *Cam* 1D 3

Beaulands Clo. *Cam* 1E **21**
Beaumont Cres. *Cam* 4C **30**
Beaumont Rd. *Cam* 4C **30**
Beche Rd. *Cam* 2F **21**
Beeches, The. *Cam* 4E **13**
Beehive Cen. *Cam* 2A **22**
Belgrave Rd. *Cam* 4B **22**
Bell Hill. *His* 2A **6**
Belmont Pl. *Cam* 2D **21** (2F **3**)
Belmore Clo. *Cam* 4B **12**
Belvoir Rd. *Cam* .1E **21**
Belvoir Ter. *Cam* .5D **21**
Benet Ct. *Mil* 5B **8**
Benet Pl. *Cam* 4D **21** (5E **3**)
Benet St. *Cam* 3C **20** (3D **3**)
Benians Ct. *Cam* .1A **20**
Bennys Way. *Cot* .2A **18**
Benson Pl. *Cam* .5B **12**
Benson St. *Cam* .5B **12**
Bentinck St. *Cam* 4D **21**
Bentinck Ter. *Cam* 4D **21**
Bentley Rd. *Cam* .2D **29**
Bergholt Clo. *Cam* 5D **15**
Bermuda Rd. *Cam* 5B **12**
Bermuda Ter. *Cam* 5B **12**
Berrylands. *Cam* .4E **13**
Beverley Way. *Cam* 4C **28**
Biggin Abbey. 1E **15**
Biggin La. *Fen D* .1E **15**
Bill Briggs Ct. *Cam* 4A **22**
Birch Clo. *Cam* 4E **13**
Bird Farm Rd. *Ful* 2D **33**
Bird Sanctuary. 1D **31**
Bird's Farm. 4A **26**
Birdwood Rd. *Cam* 1C **30**
Bishops Ct. *Cam* .5B **28**
Bishop's Rd. *Cam* 5C **28**
Bishop Way. *Imp* .3B **6**
Blackberry Clo. *Cam* 2E **13**
Blackhall Rd. *Cam* 2B **12**
Blackmoor Head Yd. *Cam* 1D **3**
Blackthorn Clo. *Cam* 3E **13**
Blackwell Cvn. Site. *Cam* 5E **7**
Blanford Wlk. *Cam* 2B **12**
Blenheim Clo. *Cam* 2D **31**
Blinco Gro. *Cam* .2F **29**
Bliss Way. *Cam* .1F **31**
Blossom St. *Cam* 3F **21**
Boathouse Ct. *Cam* 1D **21**
Borley Way. *Tev* .3A **24**
Borrowdale. *Cam* 3B **12**
Bosworth Rd. *Cam* 2C **30**
Botolph La. *Cam* 3C **20** (4D **3**)
Boundary Ct. *Cam* 1F **29**
Bourne Rd. *Cam* .4B **14**
Bowers Cft. *Cam* .4B **30**
Brackenbury. *Imp* 3B **6**
Brackley Clo. *Cam* 3C **12**
(in two parts)
Brackyn Rd. *Cam* 5A **22**
Bradrushe Fields. *Cam* 1E **19**
Bradmore Ct. Cam 3E **21**
(off Bradmore St.)
Bradmore La. *Cam* 3E **21**
Bradmore St. *Cam* 3E **21**
Bradwells Ct. *Cam* 3D **21** (3E **3**)
Brambles, The. *Cam* 5C **28**
Brambles, The. *Gir* 3E **11**
Bramley Ct. *Cam* .3B **14**
Brampton Rd. *Cam* 3A **22**
Brandon Ct. Cam .3E **21**
(off Brandon Rd.)
Brandon Pl. *Cam* .3E **21**
Braybrooke Pl. *Cam* 4E **23**
Breckenwood Rd. *Ful* 1D **33**
Brentwood Clo. *Cam* 5D **15**
Brentwood Ct. *Cam* 5D **15**
Bridewell Rd. *Cam* 1F **31**

Bridgacre. *Cam* 1E **21**
Bridge Rd. *Imp* 3B **6**
Bridge St. *Cam* 2C **20** (1D **3**)
Bridle Way. *Gran* .3E **27**
Brierley Wlk. *Cam* 2B **12**
Brimley Rd. *Cam* .3D **13**
Britannic Way. *Cam* 5E **23**
British Antarctic Survey. 1D **19**
Britten Pl. *Cam* 5C **22**
Broadmeadows. *Cam* 1E **21**
Broad St. *Cam* 3E **21**
Broadway. *Gran* 3F **27**
Broadway, The. *Cam* 4A **22**
Broadway, The. *Oak* 1B **4**
Brook Clo. *His* 3A **6**
Brookfield Rd. *Cot* 2A **18**
Brookfields. 5B **22**
Brookfields. *Cam* .4B **22**
BROOKFIELDS HOSPITAL. 4B **22**
Brooklands Av. *Cam* 1D **29**
Brooklands Ct. *Cam* 5E **21**
Brook La. *Cot* 2B **18**
Brooklyn Ct. *Cam* 2B **30**
Brookmount Ct. *Cam* 1E **13**
Brookside. *Cam* 4D **21** (5E **3**)
Brookside La. *Cam* 5D **21**
Brooks Rd. *Cam* .4B **22**
Brother's Pl. *Cam* 1C **30**
Brownlow Rd. *Cam* 3B **12**
Broxbourne Clo. *Cam* 5F **23**
Brunswick Cotts. *Cam* 2E **21**
Brunswick Ct. *Ful* .2D **33**
Brunswick Gdns. *Cam* 2E **21** (1F **3**)
Brunswick Ter. *Cam* 2E **21**
Brunswick Wlk. *Cam* 2E **21** (1F **3**)
Buchan St. *Cam* 1D **13**
Buckingham Rd. *Cam* 1B **20**
Budleigh Clo. *Cam* 5C **22**
Buffalo Way. *Cam* 5F **23**
Bullen Clo. *Cam* .2C **30**
Bulstrode Gdns. *Cam* 1F **19**
Bulteel Clo. *Mil* 3B **8**
Bunker's Hill. *Cam* 3E **11**
Burgoynes Farm Clo. *Imp* 3C **6**
Burgoynes Rd. *Imp* 3C **6**
Burkett Way. *His* 1A **6**
Burleigh Pl. *Cam* .2E **21**
Burleigh St. *Cam* .2E **21**
Burling Ct. *Cam* 1B **30**
Burling Wlk. *Mil* 3C **8**
Burnham Clo. *Cam* 1F **31**
Burnside. *Cam* 5C **22**
Burnt Clo. *Gran* 3F **27**
Burrell's Fld. *Cam* 2B **20** (2A **2**)
Burrell's Wlk. *Cam* 3B **20** (3A **2**)
Burrough Fld. *Imp* .5B **6**
Bury Ct. *Cam* 3A **22**
Butcher Clo. *Mil* 3B **8**
Butler Way. *Cam* .3C **12**
Butt La. *Mil* 3F **7**
Byron Sq. *Cam* 5C **28**

C

Cadwin Fld. *Cam* .2E **13**
Caithness Ct. *Cam* 1D **13**
Caledon Way. *Cam* 1D **13**
Callander Clo. *Cam* 2C **12**
Cambanks. *Cam* .5F **13**
Cambridge. 3C **20** (3D **3**)
Cambridge City Airport. 2E **23**
Cambridge & County Folk Mus. 1C **2**
Cambridge Bus. Pk. *Cam* 2B **14**
Cambridge City F.C. 5D **13**
CAMBRIDGE LEA BUPA HOSPITAL. 4B **6**
Cambridge Leisure Park. 1F **29**
CAMBRIDGE NUFFIELD HOSPITAL. 1D **29**

Cambridge Pl. *Cam* 4E **21**
Cambridge Retail Pk. *Cam* 2A **22**
Cambridge Rd. *Bart* 4B **26**
Cambridge Rd. *Cam & Ful* 2F **31**
Cambridge Rd. *Cax & Cot* 5A **10**
Cambridge Rd. *Gir* 5D **5**
Cambridge Rd. *Imp & Cam* 5B **6**
　　　　　　　　　　　　　　(in two parts)
Cambridge Rd. *Mil* 5B **8**
Cambridge Rd. *Oak* 1B **4**
Cambridge Rd. Ind. Est. *Mil* 5B **8**
Cambridge Rugby Football Ground.
. . . . .5F **19**
Cambridge Science Pk. *Cam* 1F **13**
Cambridge Technopark. *Cam* 1C **22**
Cambridge United F.C. (Abbey Stadium)
. . . . .1B **22**
Cambridge University Cricket Club.
. . . . .4E **21**
Cambury Ct. *Cam* 1F **13**
Cam Causeway. *Cam* 3A **14**
Camden Ct. *Cam* 3D **21** (4F **3**)
Cameron Rd. *Cam* 2D **13**
Campbell La. *Cam* 4B **28**
Campbell St. *Cam* 4A **22**
Campkin Ct. *Cam* 2E **13**
Campkin Rd. *Cam* 3D **13**
Camside. *Cam* 5F **13**
Cannon Ct. *Cam* 5F **13**
Canterbury Clo. *Cam* 5B **12**
Canterbury Rd. *Cam* 5B **12**
Canterbury St. *Cam* 5B **12**
Capstan Clo. *Cam* 1F **21**
Capuchin Ct. *Cam* 5F **23**
Caravere Clo. *Cam* 1E **13**
Caraway Rd. *Ful* 2D **33**
Caribou Way. *Cam* 5F **23**
Carisbrooke Rd. *Cam* 4B **12**
Carlton Ct. *Cam* 4C **12**
Carlton Ter. *Cam* 4C **12**
Carlton Way. *Cam* 4C **12**
Carlyle Rd. *Cam* 1C **20**
Caroline Pl. *Cam* 3E **21**
Carrick Clo. *Cam* 2D **31**
Castle Hill. 1C **20**
Castle Pk. *Cam* 1C **20**
Castle Row. *Cam* 1B **20**
Castle St. *Cam* 1B **20** (1C **2**)
Catharine St. *Cam* 4A **22**
Causeway Pas. *Cam* 2E **21**
Causewayside. *Cam* 4C **20** (5C **2**)
Cave Ind. Est. *Cam* 3C **14**
Cavendish Av. *Cam* 2F **29**
Cavendish Pl. *Cam* 3A **22**
Cavendish Rd. *Cam* 4A **22**
Cavesson St. *Cam* 3B **12**
Cedar Ct. *Cam* 4A **30**
Cenacle, The. *Cam* 5B **20**
Chalfont Clo. *Cam* 1E **31**
Chalk Gro. *Cam* 3C **30**
Chalmers Rd. *Cam* 1B **30**
Chamberlin Ct. *Cam* 5B **12**
Champneys Wlk. *Cam* 4B **20** (5A **2**)
Chancellors Wlk. *Cam* 3B **12**
Chantry Clo. *Cam* 5E **13**
Chantry, The. *Ful* 2F **33**
Chapel St. *Cam* 5F **13**
Chaplin's Clo. *Ful* 2E **33**
Chapman Ct. *Cam* 2D **13**
Charles St. *Cam* 5A **22**
Chartfield Rd. *Cam* 1E **31**
Chatsworth Av. *Cam* 4B **12**
Chaucer Clo. *Cam* 1D **29**
Chaucer Rd. *Cam* 5C **20**
Cheddar's La. *Cam* 1A **22**
Chedworth St. *Cam* 5B **20**
Chelsea M. *Cam* 5B **12**
Chelwood Rd. *Cam* 1E **31**
Cheney Way. *Cam* 4B **14**
Chequers Clo. *Cam* 2E **31**
Chequers Rd. *Imp* 4B **6**
Cherry Bounds Rd. *Gir* 1D **11**
Cherry Clo. *Cam* 2D **31**
Cherry Clo. *Mil* 3C **8**
Cherry Hinton. .2E **31**
Cherry Hinton Rd. *Cam* 5C **30**
　　　　　　　　　　　　　　(Babraham Rd.)
Cherry Hinton Rd. *Cam* 1F **29**
　　　　　　　　　　　　　　(Hills Rd.)
Cherry Hinton Rd. *Cam & Tev* 5F **23**
Cherry Orchard. *Ful* 2C **32**
Cherry Orchard. *Oak* 1B **4**
Cherwell Ct. *Cam* 5B **20**
Chesterfield Rd. *Cam* 3F **13**
Chesterton. 5F **13**
Chesterton Hall Cres. *Cam* 5E **13**
Chesterton La. *Cam* 1C **20** (1C **2**)
Chesterton Mills. *Cam* 5B **12**
Chesterton Rd. *Cam* 1C **20**
Chesterton Towers. Cam 5F **13**
　　　　　　　　　　　　　　(off Chapel St.)
Chestnut Gro. *Cam* 5E **13**
Chigwell Ct. *Cam* 5D **15**
Chivers Way. *His* 4A **6**
Christchurch St. *Cam* 2E **21**
Christ's Ct. *Cam* 3D **21** (3F **3**)
Christ's La. *Cam* 3D **21** (3E **3**)
Church End. 4F **23**
Church End. *Cam* 4E **23**
Church End. *Cot* 2A **18**
Church End. *Horn* 4F **9**
Churchfield Ct. *Gir* 4D **5**
Church La. *Bart* 3A **26**
Church La. *Cam* 5B **28**
Church La. *Ful* 2F **33**
Church La. *Gir* 1D **11**
Church La. *Mil* 4C **8**
Chu. Rate Wlk. *Cam* 4B **20** (5B **2**)
Church Rd. *Stow* 5E **17**
Church Rd. *Tev* 2A **24**
Church St. *Fen D* 4D **15**
Church St. *Cam* 5F **13**
Church St. *His* 1A **6**
Cineworld. 1F **29**
City Rd. *Cam* .3E **21**
Clare College Memorial Ct.
　　Cam 3B **20** (3B **2**)
Clare Ct. *Mil* .4C **8**
Claremont. *Cam* 5E **21**
Clarendon Rd. *Cam* 1E **29**
Clarendon St. *Cam* 3D **21** (3F **3**)
Clare Rd. *Cam* 4B **20**
Clare St. *Cam* 5B **12**
Clarkson Clo. *Cam* 2A **20** (1A **2**)
Clarkson Rd. *Cam* 2A **20** (1A **2**)
Clay Clo. La. *Imp* 3C **6**
Claygate Rd. *Cam* 1E **31**
Clayhithe Rd. *Horn* 4F **9**
Clay St. *His* 1A **6**
Clerk Maxwell Rd. *Cam* 2F **19**
Clifton Ct. *Cam* 1F **29**
Clifton Rd. *Cam* 1F **29**
Cliveden Clo. *Cam* 4B **12**
Clover Ct. *Cam* 2F **31**
Coach Ho. Ct. *Cam* 5E **13**
Cobble Yd. Cam 2E **21**
　　　　　　　　　　　　　　(off Napier St.)
Cobholm Pl. *Cam* 1E **13**
Cockburn St. *Cam* 4A **22**
Cockcroft Pl. *Cam* 2A **20** (1A **2**)
Cockerell Rd. *Cam* 4C **12**
Cockerton Rd. *Gir* 5D **5**
Coe's Ct. *Cam* 2C **30**
Coggeshall Clo. *Cam* 5D **15**
Coldhams Bus. Pk. *Cam* 4D **23**
Coldham's Gro. *Cam* 4B **22**

Coldham's La. *Cam* 2A **22**
Coldham's Rd. *Cam* 2A **22**
Coleridge Rd. *Cam* 1A **30**
Coles La. *Oak* 1B **4**
Coles Rd. *Mil* 4C **8**
College Farm Ct. *Bart* 4B **26**
College Fields. *Cam* .3E **13**
College Pk. *Cam* 5E **23**
College Rd. *Imp* 5A **6**
Collier Rd. *Cam* 3E **21**
Colliers La. *Stow* 3F **17**
Coltsfoot Clo. *Cam* 2F **31**
Colville Rd. *Cam* 1E **31**
Colwyn Clo. *Cam* 4C **12**
Comberton Rd. *Bart* .2A **26**
Comfrey Ct. *Cam* 2F **31**
Conder Clo. *Mil* 3B **8**
Conduit Head Rd. *Cam* 1E **19**
Coniston Rd. *Cam* 1A **30**
Consul Ct. *Cam* 1D **13**
Conway Clo. *Cam* 1E **31**
Cook Clo. *Cam* 3A **14**
Coppice, The. *Imp* 5B **6**
Corfe Clo. *Cam* 2F **29**
Corn Exchange St. *Cam* 3C **20** (3D **3**)
Corn Exchange Theatre. 3D **3**
Cornway, The. *Ful* 2D **33**
Corona Rd. *Cam* 5D **13**
Coronation M. *Cam* .5D **21**
Coronation Pl. *Cam* .5D **21**
Coronation St. *Cam* .4D **21**
Corrie Rd. *Cam* 5A **22**
Cosin Ct. *Cam* 4C **20** (5D **3**)
Coton. 2A **18**
Coton Footpath. *Cam* 2D **19**
Coton Rd. *Gran* 1D **27**
Cottenham Rd. *His* 1A **6**
Coulson Clo. *Mil* 4B **8**
Courtland Av. *Cam* 2B **30**
Courtney Way. *Cam* .4D **13**
Covent Garden. *Cam* 4E **21**
Cow La. *Ful* 2D **33**
Cowley Pk. *Cam* 2A **14**
Cowley Rd. *Cam* 2B **14**
Cowper Rd. *Cam* 1A **30**
Cox's Drove. *Ful* 1E **33**
Craister Ct. *Cam* 2D **13**
Crane Ind. Est. *Mil* 5C **8**
Cranleigh Clo. *Cam* .5C **28**
Cranmer Rd. *Cam* 3A **20** (4A **2**)
Crathern Way. *Cam* .2E **13**
Craven Clo. *Cam* 5C **28**
Crawford Clo. *Cam* .1D **13**
Crescent, The. *Cam* .1A **20**
Crescent, The. *Imp* 5B **6**
Crispin Clo. *Cam* 2C **12**
Crispin Pl. *Cam* 2E **21**
Croft Clo. *His* 1A **6**
Croft Gdns. *Cam* 5B **20**
Croftgate. *Cam* 5A **20**
Cft. Holme La. *Cam* .1D **21**
Croft La. *Oak* 1A **4**
Croft Lodge. *Cam* 5B **20**
Croft, The. *Ful* 2D **33**
Crome Ditch Clo. *Gran* 3F **27**
Cromwell Ct. *Cam* 2F **3**
Cromwell Rd. *Cam* 3A **22**
Crosfield Ct. *Cam* 2D **13**
Cross St. *Cam* 4E **21**
Crossways Gdns. *Cam* 5C **28**
Crossways Ho. *Cam* 5C **28**
Crowland Way. *Cam* 2E **13**
Crowthorne Clo. *Cam* 1E **31**
Cunningham Clo. *Cam* 3D **13**
Cutter Ferry Clo. *Cam* 1F **21**
Cutter Ferry La. *Cam* 1E **21**
Cutter Ferry Path. *Cam* 1E **21**
Cyprus Rd. *Cam* 5B **22**

D

Daisy Clo. *Cam* 2C **12**
Dalegarth. *Cam* 5E **13**
Dalton Sq. *Cam* 4A **14**
Dane Dri. *Cam* 3F **19**
Danesbury Ct. *Cam* .3B **22**
Darwin Dri. *Cam* 4B **12**
Davey Clo. *Imp* 3B **6**
Davey Ho. *Cam* 4F **13**
David Bull Way. *Mil* .3C **8**
David St. *Cam* 4F **21**
Davy Rd. *Cam* 5A **22**
Daws Clo. *Cam* 1E **31**
Daws La. *Cam* 1D **31**
Dean Dri. *Cam* 3A **30**
De Freville Av. *Cam* .1E **21**
Denham Pl. *Cam* 4A **22**
Denis Wilson Ct. *Cam* 3D **29**
Dennis Rd. *Cam* 5E **15**
Derby Rd. *Cam* 1A **30**
Derby St. *Cam* 5B **20**
Derwent Clo. *Cam* 2C **30**
Desmond Av. *Cam* 1E **31**
Devonshire M. *Cam* .5F **21**
Devonshire Rd. *Cam* 5F **21**
Diamond Clo. *Cam* .2D **29**
Discovery Way. *Cam* 3B **14**
Ditchburn Pl. *Cam* 4F **21**
Ditton Ct. *Cam* 5D **15**
Ditton Fields. *Cam* 1B **22**
Ditton La. *Cam & Fen D* 1D **23**
Ditton Wlk. *Cam* 5B **14**
Dock La. *Horn* 4F **9**
Doctor's Clo. *Imp* 3C **6**
Dodford La. *Gir* 4C **4**
Dogget's La. *Ful* 3E **33**
Doggett Rd. *Cam* 1D **31**
Dole, The. *Imp* 3B **6**
. . . . (in two parts)
Dolphin Clo. *Cam* 5F **23**
Douglas Ho. *Cam* 2D **29**
Dover St. *Cam* 3E **21**
Dowding Way. *Cam* .3C **12**
Downhams La. *Cam* 3E **13**
Downing Pl. *Cam* 3D **21** (4E **3**)
Downing St. *Cam* 3D **21** (4E **3**)
Drake Way. *Imp* 2C **6**
Drayton Clo. *Cam* 2F **31**
Drayton Rd. *Cam* 2F **31**
Drift, The. *Oak* 1A **4**
Drosier Rd. *Cam* 4E **21** (5F **3**)
Drove Way, The. *Lode* 1D **17**
Drummer St. *Cam* 3D **21** (3E **3**)
Dry Drayton Rd. *Oak* 2A **4**
Duck End. *Gir* 1D **11**
Dudley Rd. *Cam* 5C **14**
Dundee Clo. *Cam* 4F **13**
Dunmowe Way. *Ful* .2D **33**
Dunsmore Clo. *Cam* 5D **15**
Durnford Way. *Cam* .4D **13**
Dwyer-Joyce Clo. *His* 2A **6**

E

Eachard Rd. *Cam* 4A **12**
Earl St. *Cam* 3D **21** (3F **3**)
Eastfield. *Cam* 4F **13**
E. Hertford St. *Cam* .1C **20**
East Rd. *Cam* 3E **21**
Eaton Clo. *Cam* 3F **13**
Edendale Clo. *Cam* .2B **30**
Eden St. *Cam* 3E **21** (3F **3**)
Eden St. Backway. *Cam* 2E **21** (2F **3**)
Edgecombe. *Cam* 2E **13**

Edinburgh Rd. *Cam* 4F **13**
Edmund Clo. *Mil* 4B **8**
Edward St. *Cam* 3F **21**
Edwinstowe Clo. *Cam* 1C **28**
Egerton Clo. *Cam* 5C **14**
Egerton Rd. *Cam* 5D **15**
Eights Marina, The. *Cam* 1F **21**
Ekin Rd. *Cam* 5C **14**
Ekin Wlk. *Cam* 5C **14**
Eland Way. *Cam* 5F **23**
Elder Clo. *Cam* 3E **13**
Elfleda Rd. *Cam* 1B **22**
Elizabeth Way. *Cam* .5E **13**
Ellesmere Rd. *Cam* 3C **12**
Ellis Ho. *Cam* 4E **13**
Ellison Clo. *Cam* 2C **12**
Elmfield Clo. *Cam* 4F **13**
Elmfield Rd. *Cam* 4F **13**
Elms, The. *Mil* 4B **8**
Elm St. *Cam* 2D **21** (2F **3**)
Elsworth Pl. *Cam* 1F **29**
Eltisley Av. *Cam* 5B **20**
Ely Pl. *Cam* 4C **28**
Ely Rd. *Mil & W'bch* 4C **8**
Emery Rd. *Cam* 3F **21**
Emery St. *Cam* 3F **21**
Emmanuel Rd. *Cam* 3D **21** (3F **3**)
Emmanuel St. *Cam* 3D **21** (3E **3**)
Emperor Ct. *Cam* 2D **13**
Ennisdale Clo. *Cam* .2D **13**
Enniskillen Rd. *Cam* .4A **14**
Epworth St. *Cam* 2D **21** (2F **3**)
Erasmus Clo. *Cam* 4C **12**
Essex Clo. *Cam* 4D **13**
Etheldred Ho. *His* 1A **6**
Evening Ct. *Cam* 2E **21**
Evergreens. *Cam* 4A **14**
Exeter Clo. *Cam* 5C **28**

F

Fairbairn Rd. *Cam* 4B **14**
Fairfax Rd. *Cam* 3A **22**
Fair St. *Cam* 2E **21** (2F **3**)
Fairway. *Gir* 4D **5**
Fallowfield. *Cam* 4A **14**
Fanshawe Rd. *Cam* .1F **29**
Farmers Row. *Ful* 3D **33**
Farmstead Clo. *His* 1A **6**
Farringford Clo. *Cam* 3B **12**
Faulkner Clo. *Mil* 4B **8**
Fazeley Ho. *Cam* 2F **21**
(off East Rd.)
Felton St. *Cam* 4F **21**
Fen Causeway, The. *Cam* 4C **20** (5C **2**)
Fen Ditton. 4D **15**
Fendon Clo. *Cam* 4A **30**
Fendon Rd. *Cam* 4A **30**
Fen Drove Way. *Tev* .4D **25**
Fennec Clo. *Cam* 5A **24**
Fenners Lawn. *Cam* .4E **21**
Fen Rd. *Cam* 4B **14**
Fen Rd. *Mil* 4C **8**
Ferndale. *Tev* 4B **24**
Ferndale Ri. *Cam* 5B **14**
Fernlea Clo. *Cam* 5E **23**
Ferrars Way. *Cam* 3C **12**
Ferry La. *Cam* 5A **14**
Ferry Path. *Cam* 1D **21**
Field La. *Fen D* 2D **15**
Field Way. *Cam* 4B **30**
Finch Rd. *Cam* 4C **12**
Fisher's La. *Cam* 1E **31**
Fisher St. *Cam* 1C **20**
Fison Rd. *Cam* 5D **15**
Fitzroy La. *Cam* 2E **21** (2F **3**)
Fitzroy St. *Cam* 2E **21** (2F **3**)

Fitzwilliam Mus. 4C **20** (5D **3**)
Fitzwilliam Rd. *Cam* 1E **29**
Fitzwilliam St. *Cam* 4D **21** (5E **3**)
Flamsteed Rd. *Cam* .1F **29**
Fletcher's Ter. *Cam* 4F **21**
Flower St. *Cam* 3F **21**
Fontwell Av. *Cam* 3B **12**
Footpath, The. *Cot* 2B **18**
Footpath, The. *Gran* .3F **27**
Fordwich Clo. *Cam* 3C **12**
Forest Rd. *Cam* 2D **31**
Fortescue Rd. *Cam* .3D **13**
Forum Ct. *Cam* 2D **13**
Foster Rd. *Cam* 5C **28**
Fox's Clo. *Mil* 4C **8**
Francis Darwin Ct. *Cam* 4B **12**
Francis Pas. *Cam* 5D **21**
Franks La. *Cam* 4A **14**
Fraser Rd. *Cam* 3F **13**
Free School La. *Cam* 3C **20** (3D **3**)
French's Rd. *Cam* 5C **12**
Friar's Clo. *Cam* 2E **31**
Froment Way. *Mil* 3B **8**
Fromont Clo. *Ful* 3D **33**
Fulbourn. 2E **33**
FULBOURN HOSPITAL. 2A **32**
Fulbourn Old Drift. *Cam* 5F **23**
(in three parts)
Fulbourn Rd. *Cam* 2E **31**
Fulbourn Rd. *Tev* 4B **24**
Fulbrooke Rd. *Cam* 5A **20**
Fuller Way. *Cam* 1A **20**

G

Gainsborough Clo. *Cam* 3A **14**
Galfrid Rd. *Cam* 2C **22**
Garden Wlk. *Cam* 5C **12**
Garden Wlk. *His* 1B **6**
Garlic Row. *Cam* 1A **22**
Garner Clo. *Mil* 3B **8**
Garret Hostel La. *Cam* 2B **20** (3B **2**)
Garry Dri. *Cam* 2F **13**
Gayton Clo. *Cam* 4C **28**
Gazeley Rd. *Cam* 3C **28**
Gazelle Way. *Cam* 4F **23**
Geldart St. *Cam* 2F **21**
Geoffrey Bishop Av. *Ful* 3E **33**
George IV St. *Cam* 4E **21** (5F **3**)
George Nuttall Clo. *Cam* 3F **13**
George Pateman Ct. *Cam* 5E **21**
Georges Ter. *Cam* 5B **12**
George St. *Cam* 5E **13**
Gerard Clo. *Cam* 1C **22**
Gerard Rd. *Cam* 1C **22**
Gifford Pl. *Cam* 2C **20** (2D **3**)
Gifford's Clo. *Gir* 1D **11**
Gilbert Clo. *Cam* 4B **12**
Gilbert Rd. *Cam* 4B **12**
Gilmerton Ct. *Cam* 3C **28**
Girton. 4D **5**
Girton Rd. *Gir* 1E **11**
Gisborne Rd. *Cam* 1B **30**
Gladstone Way. *Cam* .2E **31**
Glebe Rd. *Cam* 3A **30**
Glebe Way. *His* 2B **6**
Glenacre Clo. *Cam* 2D **31**
Glendale. *Mil* 5B **8**
Glenmere Clo. *Cam* 2C **30**
Glenoven Ct. *Cam* 1C **20**
(off Searle St.)
Glenville Clo. *Tev* 3A **24**
Glisson Rd. *Cam* 4E **21**
Godesdone Rd. *Cam* .2F **21**
Goding Way. *Mil* 4D **9**
Godwin Clo. *Cam* 3B **30**
Godwin Way. *Cam* 3B **30**

Gog Magog Golf Course—Holben Clo.

Gog Magog Golf Course. 5E 31
Golding Rd. *Cam* .5A 22
Gonville Pl. *Cam* 4E 21 (5F 3)
Gough Way. *Cam* .4F 19
Gowers, The. *Gir* .5D 5
Grafton Cen. *Cam* 2E 21
Grafton St. *Cam* .2E 21
Grandridge Clo. *Ful* 3E 33
Grange Ct. *Cam* 4A 20 (5A 2)
Grange Dri. *Gir* 2D 11
Grange Gdns. *Cam* 4A 20 (5A 2)
Grange Rd. *Cam* 4A 20 (5A 2)
Granham's Rd. *Cam* 5B 30
Granta Pl. *Cam* 4C 20 (4C 2)
Grantchester. 3F 27
Grantchester Meadows. *Cam* 5B 20
Grantchester Rd. *Cot* 3B 18
Grantchester Rd. *Gran* 2F 27
Grantchester Rd. *Gran & Cam* 4A 28
Grantchester St. *Cam* 5B 20
Grasmere Gdns. *Cam* 1C 20
Grayling Clo. *Cam* 5F 13
Gray Rd. *Cam* 1C 30
Great Clo. *Bart* 3A 26
Gt. Eastern St. *Cam* 4A 22
Greater Foxes. *Ful* 2E 33
Green End. *Fen D* 3D 15
Grn. End Rd. *Cam* 3A 14
Greenlands. *Cam* .4A 30
Greenleas. *His* 1A 6
Green Pk. *Cam* 3A 14
Green's Rd. *Cam* .5D 13
Green St. *Cam* 2C 20 (2D 3)
Green, The. *Cam* .4A 14
Gresham Rd. *Cam* 4E 21 (5F 3)
Gretton Ct. *Gir* 5C 4
Greville Rd. *Cam* .5A 22
Greystoke Ct. *Cam* 2D 31
Greystoke Rd. *Cam* 2D 31
Grieve Ct. *Cam* 4B 14
Grove, The. *Cam* .3A 14
Guest Rd. *Cam* 3E 21
Guildhall Pl. *Cam* 3D 21 (3D 3)
Guildhall St. *Cam* 3C 20 (3D 3)
Gunhild Clo. *Cam* 2C 30
Gunhild Ct. *Cam* .2B 30
Gunhild Way. *Cam* 2B 30
Gunnell Clo. *Mil* .4C 8
Gunning Way. *Cam* 3C 12
Gun's La. *His* 1F 5
Gurney Way. *Cam* 5D 13
Gwydir St. *Cam* 3F 21

H

Hadleigh Ct. *Cam* 5D 15
Haggis Gap. *Ful* .3E 33
Haig Ct. *Cam* 5F 13
Hale Av. *Cam* 5C 12
Hale St. *Cam* 1C 20
Half Acre. *Mil* 4B 8
Halifax Rd. *Cam* .5A 12
Hall End. *Mil* 4C 8
Hall Farm Rd. *Cam* 4C 12
Hamilton Rd. *Cam* 1E 21
Hanover Ct. *Cam* .4E 21
(off Coronation St.)
Hanson Ct. *Cam* .2D 13
Harcombe Rd. *Cam* 1D 31
Harding Way. *Cam* 3B 12
Harding Way. *His* .2A 6
Hardwick St. *Cam* 5B 20
Harebell Clo. *Cam* 2F 31
Harris Rd. *Cam* 3C 12
Harry Scott Ct. *Cam* 2D 13
Harshel Courts. *Cam* 2A 30
Hartington Gro. *Cam* 2F 29

Harvest Way. *Cam* 2F 21
Harvey Goodwin Av. *Cam* 5C 12
Harvey Goodwin Ct. *Cam* 5C 12
Harvey Goodwin Gdns. *Cam* 5C 12
Harvey Rd. *Cam* 4E 21 (5F 3)
Haslingfield Rd. *Bart* 5A 26
Hatherdene Clo. *Cam* 4D 23
Hauxton Rd. *Cam* 5B 28
Havenfield. *Cam* .4E 13
Haven, The. *Ful* 2E 33
Haviland Way. *Cam* 3E 13
Hawkins Rd. *Cam* 2E 13
Hawthorn Way. *Cam* 5E 13
Haymarket Rd. *Cam* 1B 20 (1B 2)
Hayster Dri. *Cam* .1D 31
Haytor. *Mil* 4B 8
Hazelwood Clo. *Cam* 2B 12
Headford Clo. *Cam* 5C 14
Headington Clo. *Cam* 2E 31
Headington Dri. *Cam* 2E 31
Heath Ho. *Cam* 4F 13
Hedgerley Clo. *Cam* 1F 19
Helen Clo. *Cam* 5D 15
Hemingford Rd. *Cam* 4A 22
Henley Rd. *Cam* .2A 22
Henry Morris Rd. *Imp* 3B 6
Herbert St. *Cam* .5D 13
Herbert Twin Ct. *Cam* 5C 14
Hercules Clo. *Cam* 1D 13
Hereward Clo. *Imp* 3B 6
Hereward Ho. *Cam* 2A 32
Heron's Clo. *Cam* .3C 30
Herring's Clo. *Stow* 4F 17
Herschel Rd. *Cam* 3A 20 (3A 2)
Hertford St. *Cam* .1C 20
Hester Adrian Way. *Cam* 5E 13
Hick's La. *Gir* 1D 11
High Cross. 2D 19
Highdene Rd. *Cam* 1F 31
High Ditch Rd. *Fen D* 4E 15
Highfield Av. *Cam* 4D 13
Highfield Ga. *Ful* .1E 33
Highfield Rd. *Imp* .5B 6
Highsett. *Cam* 5E 21
High St. *Fen D* 4D 15
High St. *Bart* 3A 26
High St. *Cam* (CB1) 2E 31
High St. *Cam* (CB2) 5C 28
High St. *Cam* (CB4) 5F 13
High St. *Cot* 2A 18
High St. *Ful* 2E 33
High St. *Gir* 5D 5
High St. *Gran* 3F 27
High St. *His* 2A 6
High St. *Horn* 5F 9
High St. *Land* 1C 8
High St. *Mil* 4C 8
High St. *Oak* 1B 4
High St. *Tev* 3A 24
Highworth Av. *Cam* 4E 13
Hilda St. *Cam* 5C 12
Hilderstone Ho. Cam 2F 21
(off Staffordshire St.)
Hills Av. *Cam* 2F 29
Hills Rd. *Cam* 4E 21 (5F 3)
Hind Loders. *Ful* .4F 33
Hines Clo. *Bart* 3A 26
Hinton Av. *Cam* 2B 30
Hinton Rd. *Ful* 2C 32
Histon. 2A 6
Histon Footpath. *Gir* 4E 5
Histon Rd. *Cam* 2B 12
Hoadly Rd. *Cam* .4A 12
Hobart Rd. *Cam* .5A 22
(in two parts)
Hobson's Pas. *Cam* 2D 21 (2E 3)
Hobson St. *Cam* 2D 21 (2E 3)
Holben Clo. *Bart* .4A 26

Holbrook Rd. *Cam* 3A **30**
Holland St. *Cam* 1C **30**
Hollmans Clo. *Ful* 3E **33**
Holme Clo. *Oak* 1B **4**
Holyoake Ct. *Cam* 1B **22**
Holyrood Clo. *Cam* 3B **12**
Home Clo. *His* 3A **6**
Home Clo. *W Wick* 2D **33**
Home End. *Ful* 3F **33**
Homefield Clo. *Imp* 3B **6**
Homerton Ct. *Cam* 2F **29**
Homerton St. *Cam* 1F **29**
Homing, The. *Cam* 1D **23**
Honey Hill. *Cam* 1B **20** (1B **2**)
Honey Hill M. *Cam* 1B **20** (1B **2**)
Hooper St. *Cam* .3F **21**
Hope St. *Cam* 4A **22**
Hope St. Yd. *Cam* 4A **22**
Hopkins Clo. *Cam* 3F **13**
Horningsea. 4F **9**
Horningsea Rd. *Fen D* 4E **15**
Howard Clo. *Cam* 5C **14**
Howard Ct. *Cam* 5D **15**
Howard Rd. *Cam* 5C **14**
Howes Pl. *Cam* .4F **11**
Howgate Rd. *Cam* 2B **12**
Hulatt Rd. *Cam* .3B **30**
Humberstone Rd. *Cam* 1E **21**
Humphreys Rd. *Cam* 3D **13**
Humphries Way. *Mil* 4C **8**
Huntingdon Rd. *Gir* 2D **11**
Huntley Clo. *Cam* 5D **15**
Huntsmill. *Ful* 3D **33**
Hurrell Rd. *Cam* 3B **12**
Hurst Pk. Av. *Cam* 4D **13**
Hyde Pk. Corner. *Cam* 4D **21** (5F **3**)

I

IDA DARWIN HOSPITAL. 2C **32**
Impala Dri. *Cam* 5A **24**
Impett's La. *Ful* .3F **33**
Impington. 4B **6**
Impington La. *His* 3B **6**
Inverness Clo. *Cam* 4F **13**
Iver Clo. *Cam* 5E **23**
Ivy Fld. *Bart* 3A **26**
Izaak Walton Way. *Cam* 4B **14**

J

Jackson Rd. *Cam* 2F **13**
Jack Warren Grn. *Cam* 1E **23**
James Carlton Clo. *Mil* 5B **8**
James St. *Cam* .2E **21**
Jasmine Ct. *Cam* 2B **30**
Jedburgh Clo. *Cam* 2C **12**
Jedburgh Ct. *Cam* 2D **13**
Jeeves Acre. *Ful* 3F **33**
Jermyn Clo. *Cam* 3C **12**
Jesus Clo. *Cam* 2D **21** (1F **3**)
Jesus La. *Cam* 2C **20** (2D **3**)
Jesus Ter. *Cam* 2E **21** (2F **3**)
JJ Thompson Av. *Cam* 2E **19**
John Clarke Ct. *Cam* 4E **13**
John Conder Ct. *Cam* 5B **22**
John St. *Cam* 3E **21**
Jolley Way. *Cam* 2E **13**
Jordan's Yd. *Cam* 1D **3**
Junction, The. 1F **29**

K

Kaldor Ct. *Cam* .2D **13**
(off Buchan St.)

Kathleen Elliott Way. *Cam* 5E **23**
Kay Hitch Way. *His* 4B **6**
Keates Rd. *Cam* 2F **31**
Kelsey Cres. *Cam* 5F **23**
Kelsey Kerridge Sports Hall. 3E **21**
Kelvin Clo. *Cam* 2C **30**
Kendal Ct. *Imp* 4B **6**
Kendal Way. *Cam* 3A **14**
Kensington Ct. *Cam* 1C **22**
(off Quainton Clo.)
Ken's Way. *Mil* 4C **8**
Kent Way. *Cam* .2E **13**
Kerridge Clo. *Cam* 3F **21**
Kettles Clo. *Oak* .1B **4**
Kettles Yard. 1B **2**
Kettles Yd. *Cam* 1C **20** (1C **2**)
Keynes Rd. *Cam* 5C **14**
Kilmaine Clo. *Cam* 1E **13**
Kimberley Rd. *Cam* 1E **21**
Kings Gro. *Bart* .3A **26**
King's Hedges. 2E **13**
King's Hedges Rd. *Cam* 2B **12**
(in two parts)
King's La. *Cam* 3C **20** (4C **2**)
King's Pde. *Cam* 3C **20** (3D **3**)
King's Rd. *Cam* .5A **20**
Kingston St. *Cam* 4F **21**
King St. *Cam* 2D **21** (2E **3**)
Kingsway. *Cam* .3C **12**
Kingsway. *His* 2A **6**
Kinnaird Way. *Cam* 3B **30**
Kinross M. *Cam* .4F **13**
Kinross Rd. *Cam* 4E **13**
Kirkby Clo. *Cam* 4E **13**
Kirkwood Rd. *Cam* 1E **13**
Knight's Way. *Mil* 3C **8**
(in two parts)

L

Laburnum Clo. *Cam* 5E **13**
Lady Jane Ct. *Cam* 2F **29**
Lady Margaret Rd. *Cam* 1B **20** (1B **2**)
Lambourn Clo. *Cam* 4C **28**
Lammas Ct. *Cam* 5B **20**
Lammas Fld. *Cam* 5B **20**
Landbeach. 1C **8**
Landbeach Rd. *Land* 1C **8**
(in two parts)
Lander Clo. *Mil* 3B **8**
Langdale Clo. *Cam* 5F **23**
Langham Rd. *Cam* 1B **30**
Lansdowne Rd. *Cam* 1E **19**
Lantree Cres. *Cam* 5C **28**
Larchfield. *Cam* .4A **20**
Larkin Clo. *Cam* .3F **13**
Larmor Dri. *Cam* 1A **20**
Latham Clo. *Cam* 1C **28**
Latham Rd. *Cam* 1C **28**
Latimer Clo. *Cam* 1D **23**
Laundress La. *Cam* 3C **20** (4C **2**)
Laundry La. *Cam* 2C **30**
Lauriston Pl. *Cam* 1D **13**
Lavender Rd. *Cam* 2F **13**
Lawns, The. *Cam* 2F **19**
Lawrence Clo. *Gir* 1D **11**
Lawrence Way. *Cam* 2E **13**
Laxton Way. *Cam* 3B **14**
Lea Ct. *Mil* 4C **8**
Lee Seng Tee Library. 4A **20**
Lees Way. *Gir* 5D **5**
Leete Rd. *Cam* .2E **31**
Legion Ct. *Cam* .2D **13**
Lemur Dri. *Cam* .5A **24**
Lensfield Rd. *Cam* 4D **21** (5E **3**)
Lents Way. *Cam* 4B **14**
Leonard Clo. *Cam* 5D **15**

Lexington Clo. *Cam* 4B **12**
Leyburn Clo. *Cam* 5F **23**
Leys Av. *Cam* 3D **13**
Leys Rd. *Cam* 4E **13**
Lichfield Rd. *Cam* 1A **30**
Lilac Ct. *Cam* 2B **30**
Lilley Clo. *Cam* 4A **14**
Limekiln Close Nature Reserve. 2E **31**
Limekiln Rd. *Cam* 4D **31**
Lime Tree Clo. *Cam* 2C **30**
Linden Clo. *Cam* 5B **12**
Lingholme Clo. *Cam* 4B **12**
Lingrey Ct. *Cam* 5C **28**
Lion Yd. *Cam* 3D **21** (3E **3**)
Lisa Ct. *Cam* 4A **14**
Lisle Wlk. *Cam* 1F **31**
Lit. St Mary's La. *Cam* 4C **20** (5D **3**)
Livermore Clo. *Cam* 2E **13**
Llandaff Chambers. *Cam* 4E **3**
Logans Way. *Cam* 1F **21**
Lone Tree Av. *Imp* 1B **12**
Lone Tree Gro. *Imp* 1B **12**
Long Drove Way. *Tev* .1E **25**
Long Reach Rd. *Cam* .4B **14**
Long Rd. *Cam* 3C **28**
Longstanton Rd. *Oak* 1A **4**
Longworth Av. *Cam* 5F **13**
Loris Ct. *Cam* 5A **24**
Loughton Ct. *Cam* 1E **23**
Love La. *Cam* 1E **31**
Lovell Rd. *Cam* 2F **13**
Love's Clo. *His* 4B **6**
Lowbury Cres. *Oak* 1A **4**
Lwr. Park St. *Cam* 2C **20** (1D **3**)
Low Fen Droveway. *Fen D* 1F **15**
Luard Clo. *Cam* 3F **29**
Luard Rd. *Cam* 2F **29**
Lucerne Clo. *Cam* 1F **31**
Lucketts Clo. *His* 1A **6**
Ludlow La. *Ful* 2F **33**
Lyndewode Rd. *Cam* .4E **21**
Lyndhurst Clo. *Mil* 4B **8**
Lynfield La. *Cam* 5F **13**
Lynx, The. *Cam* 5F **23**

M

Macfarlane Clo. *Imp* 4B **6**
Mackenzie Rd. *Cam* 3F **21**
Madingley Rd. *Cam* 1C **18** (1A **2**)
Madras Rd. *Cam* 5B **22**
Magdalene St. *Cam* 1C **20** (1C **2**)
Magnolia Clo. *Cam* 2A **30**
Magrath Av. *Cam* 1C **20**
Maid's Causeway. *Cam* 2E **21** (1F **3**)
Mailes Clo. *Bart* 3A **26**
Main St. *Stow* 4F **17**
Maio Rd. *Cam* 3E **13**
Maitland Av. *Cam* 3A **14**
Malcolm Pl. *Cam* 2D **21** (2E **3**)
Malcolm St. *Cam* 2D **21** (1E **3**)
Malden Clo. *Cam* 1C **22**
Mallards, The. *Cam* 1F **21**
Malletts Rd. *Cam* 2F **31**
Malta Rd. *Cam* 4A **22**
Malting La. *Cam* 4B **20** (5B **2**)
Maltster's Way. *Cam* 5F **13**
Malvern Rd. *Cam* 1D **31**
Mander Way. *Cam* 2B **30**
Mandrill Clo. *Cam* 5F **23**
Maners Way. *Cam* 3B **30**
Manhattan Dri. *Cam* 1E **21**
Manor Ct. *Cam* 4A **20**
Mnr. Farm Clo. *Oak* 1B **4**
Mnr. Farm Rd. *Gir* 4D **5**
Manor Pk. *His* 2F **5**
Manor Pl. *Cam* 2D **21** (2E **3**)

Manor St. *Cam* 2D **21** (2E **3**)
Manor Wlk. *Ful* 2F **33**
Mansel Ct. *Cam* 3D **13**
Mansel Way. *Cam* 3D **13**
Mansfield Clo. *Mil* 4B **8**
Mansfield Ct. *Cam* 5F **13**
Maple Clo. *Cam* 4E **13**
Maples, The. *Ful* 2D **33**
March La. *Cam* 4E **23**
March's Clo. *Ful* 2D **33**
Marfield Ct. *Cam* 4E **13**
Mariner's Way. *Cam* 1F **21**
Marion Clo. *Cam* 5A **12**
Maris La. *Cam* 5B **28**
Market Hill. *Cam* 3C **20** (3D **3**)
Market Pas. *Cam* 2C **20** (2D **3**)
Market Ri. *Cam* 1F **29**
Market St. *Cam* 2C **20** (2D **3**)
Markham Clo. *Cam* 2F **13**
Marks Way. *Gir* 5E **5**
Marlborough Ct. *Cam* .4A **20**
Marlowe Rd. *Cam* 5B **20**
Marmora Rd. *Cam* 5A **22**
Marshall Rd. *Cam* 2F **29**
Marshall's Clo. *Tev* 3A **24**
Marshall Way, The. *Cam* 1E **23**
Martingale Clo. *Cam* 3B **12**
Martin's Stile La. *Cam* .5F **13**
Mawson Rd. *Cam* 4E **21**
Mayfield Rd. *Gir* 1E **11**
Mayflower Ho. *Cam* 1E **21**
Mays Way. *Cam* 4B **14**
Meadow Cft. *Cam* (CB2) 2D **29**
Meadowcroft. Cam (CB4) 5F **13**
                                      (off Church St.)
Mdw. Farm Clo. *Oak* 1C **4**
Meadowlands Rd. *Cam* 1D **23**
Mead Vw. *Oak* 1A **4**
Megabowl. 1F **29**
Melbourne Pl. *Cam* 3E **21** (3F **3**)
Melvin Way. *His* 2F **5**
Mercers Row. *Cam* 5A **14**
Mere Way. *Cam* 3D **13**
Mere Way. *Mil* 5E **7**
Merton Rd. *His* 3A **6**
Merton St. *Cam* 5B **20**
Metcalfe Rd. *Cam* 4C **12**
Michaelmas Pl. *Cam* 5C **12**
Michaels Clo. *Gir* 5D **5**
Midhurst Clo. *Cam* 5A **14**
Midsummer Ct. *Cam* 1E **21**
Midwinter Pl. *Cam* 5E **13**
Milford St. *Cam* 3F **21**
Millcroft Ct. *Cam* 4A **22**
Mill End Clo. *Cam* 2E **31**
Mill End Rd. *Cam* 1D **31**
Millers Yd. *Cam* 3C **20** (4D **3**)
Millington La. *Cam* 5B **20**
Millington Rd. *Cam* 5A **20**
Mill La. *Cam* 3C **20** (4C **2**)
Mill La. *His* 2B **6**
Mill La. *Lin* 3F **33**
Mill Rd. *Cam* 3E **21**
Mill Rd. *Imp* 5A **6**
Mill St. *Cam* 4E **21**
Mill Way. *Gran* 4F **27**
Milton. 4C **8**
Milton Ct. *Mil* 4C **8**
MILTON HOSPICE (EAST ANGLIA'S
                             CHILDRENS HOSPICES)
                                        .4D **9**
Milton Pk. Vis. Cen., The. 5C **8**
Milton Rd. *Cam* 5D **13**
Milton Rd. *Imp* 3C **6**
Miltons Wlk. *Cam* 2D **21** (2E **3**)
Minerva Way. *Cam* 1D **13**
Miniature Railway. 5F **19**
Minter Clo. *Stow* 4F **17**

Missleton Ct. *Cam* 2B **30**
Misty Meadows. *Cam* 5C **14**
Molewood Clo. *Cam* 3B **12**
Moncrieff Clo. *Cam* 2D **13**
Monkswell. *Cam* 4C **28**
Montague Rd. *Cam* .5E **13**
Montfort Way. *Cam* .3D **13**
Montgomery Rd. *Cam* 3D **13**
Montreal Rd. *Cam* 5B **22**
Montreal Sq. *Cam* 5B **22**
Montrose Clo. *Cam* .2D **13**
Moore Clo. *Cam* 3F **13**
Mortimer Rd. *Cam* 3E **21**
Mortlock Av. *Cam* 3A **14**
Moss Bank. *Cam* 4B **14**
Mount Pleasant. *Cam* 1B **20**
Mt. Pleasant Wlk. *Cam* 1B **20**
Mowbray Rd. *Cam* 3B **30**
Mowlam Clo. *Imp* 4B **6**
Moyne Clo. *Cam* 2D **13**
Mulberry Clo. *Cam* .4E **13**
Mumford Theatre. 3F **21**
Muncey Wlk. *His* 1A **6**
Mus. of Archaeology & Anthropology.
. . . . .3D **21** (4E **3**)
Mus. of Classical Archaeology. 4B **20** (5B **2**)
Mus. of Technology. 1A **22**
Mus. of Zoology. 4D **3**
Musgrave Way. *Fen D* 3E **15**

N

Napier St. *Cam* 2E **21**
Narrow Clo. *His* 1B **6**
Narrow La. *His* 2A **6**
Natal Rd. *Cam* 5B **22**
Nature Reserve. 5E **31**
Neale Clo. *Cam* 5E **23**
Neath Farm Bus. Pk. *Cam* 5E **23**
Negus Yd. *Cam* 1E **29**
Nelson Clo. *Cam* 2F **21**
Neptune Clo. *Cam* 2D **13**
Netherhall Way. *Cam* 3C **30**
Neville Rd. *Cam* 1B **30**
New Chesterton. 3D **13**
New Ct. *Cam* 5F **13**
Newell Wlk. *Cam* 5E **23**
Newmarket Rd. *Cam & Tev* 2E **21**
Newmarket Rd. *Stow* 5E **17**
Newnham. 3A **20**
Newnham College. 4B **20** (5A **2**)
Newnham Croft. 5B **20**
Newnham Cft. St. *Cam* 5B **20**
Newnham Path. *Cam* 4B **20** (5B **2**)
Newnham Rd. *Cam* 4B **20** (5B **2**)
Newnham Ter. *Cam* 4C **20** (5C **2**)
Newnham Wlk. *Cam* 4B **20** (5B **2**)
New Pk. St. *Cam* 1C **20** (1D **3**)
New Rd. *Bart* 3A **26**
New Rd. *Imp* 4B **6**
New Rd. *Oak* 2D **5**
New School Rd. *His* .3A **6**
New Sq. *Cam* 2E **21** (2F **3**)
New St. *Cam* 2F **21**
Newton Rd. *Cam* 1D **29**
Newtown. 5D **21**
Nicholson Way. *Cam* 3D **13**
Nightingale Av. *Cam* 4A **30**
Norfolk St. *Cam* 3F **21**
Norfolk Ter. *Cam* 3F **21**
Normanhurst. *Cam* .1A **30**
Normanton Way. *His* .1A **6**
Norman Way. *Cam* 5D **23**
Northampton St. *Cam* 1B **20** (1B **2**)
North Cotts. *Cam* 3C **28**
Northfield. *Ful* 2F **33**
Northfield. *Gir* 4D **5**

Northfields Av. *Cam* .2D **13**
North St. *Cam* 5B **12**
North Ter. *Cam* 2E **21** (1F **3**)
Northumberland Clo. *Cam* 3D **13**
Norton Clo. *Cam* 1C **22**
Norwich St. *Cam* 5D **21**
Nuffield Clo. *Cam* 2B **14**
Nuffield Rd. *Cam* 3A **14**
Nun's Orchard. *His* 1A **6**
Nuns Way. *Cam* 2E **13**
Nursery Wlk. *Cam* 4B **12**
Nutter's Clo. *Gran* 3F **27**
Nuttings Rd. *Cam* 3C **22**

O

Oakington. 1B **4**
Oakington Rd. *Gir* 3D **5**
Oakley Ter. *Cam* 1E **31**
Oaks, The. *Mil* 4B **8**
Oak Tree Av. *Cam* 5E **13**
Oak Tree Way. *His* 3A **6**
Oast Ho., The. *Cam* 4A **20** (5A **2**)
Oates Way. *His* 1A **6**
Occupation Rd. *Cam* 2F **21**
Old Farm Clo. *His* 1A **6**
Old School La. *Mil* 4C **8**
Ongar Ct. *Cam* 5E **15**
Orchard Av. *Cam* 4D **13**
Orchard Clo. *Gir* 5D **5**
Orchard Dri. *Gir* 2D **11**
Orchard End. *Mil* 5B **8**
Orchard Est. *Cam* 5E **23**
Orchard Rd. *His* 1B **6**
Orchards, The. *Cam* .2E **31**
Orchard St. *Cam* 2D **21** (2F **3**)
Orchard St. *Stow* 4E **17**
Orchard Way. *Oak* 1B **4**
Orwell Furlong. *Cam* 2B **14**
Oslar's Way. *Ful* 2D **33**
Owlstone Rd. *Cam* .5B **20**
Oxford Rd. *Cam* 5A **12**
Oyster Row. *Cam* 1A **22**

P

Paddock Clo. *Imp* 2B **6**
Paddocks, The. *Cam* 2B **30**
(Cherry Hinton Rd.)
Paddocks, The. *Cam* 3B **22**
(Coldham's La.)
Paddocks Trad. Est., The. *Cam* 1B **30**
Pages Clo. *His* 2A **6**
Paget Clo. *Cam* 5D **29**
Paget Rd. *Cam* 5C **28**
Pakenham Clo. *Cam* 4F **13**
Palmers Wlk. *Cam* 3E **21**
Pamplin Ct. *Cam* 1E **31**
Panther Way. *Cam* 5F **23**
Panton St. *Cam* 4D **21** (5F **3**)
Paradise St. *Cam* 2E **21**
Park Av. *His* 2F **5**
Park Dri. *Imp* 3B **6**
Parker's Ter. *Cam* 2F **21**
Parker St. *Cam* 3D **21** (3F **3**)
Park La. *His* 2E **5**
Park Pde. *Cam* 1C **20** (1D **3**)
Parkside. *Cam* 3E **21** (3F **3**)
Parkside Pool. 3E **21**
Park St. *Cam* 2C **20** (1D **3**)
Park Ter. *Cam* 3D **21** (4F **3**)
Parlour Clo. *His* 1A **6**
Parr Clo. *Imp* 3B **6**
Parsonage St. *Cam* .2E **21**
Parsons Ct. *Cam* 3C **20** (3D **3**)
Peacock Way. *His* 1A **6**

Peakes Ct. *Cot* .2B **18**
Pearce Clo. *Cam* 4A **20**
Pearce's Yd. *Gran* 3F **27**
Pearmain Ct. *Cam* 4B **14**
Pearson Clo. *Mil* .5C **8**
Pearson Ct. *Mil* 5C **8**
Pease Way. *His* 2E **5**
Peas Hill. *Cam* 3C **20** (3D **3**)
Pelham Ct. *Cam* .3B **12**
Pemberton Pl. *Cam* 4D **21**
Pemberton Ter. *Cam* 4D **21**
Pembroke College Sports Ground. 5A **20**
Pembroke Pl. *Mil* .4C **8**
Pembroke St. *Cam* 3C **20** (4D **3**)
Pembroke Way. *Tev* 3A **24**
Penarth Pl. *Cam* .4F **19**
Pen Clo. *Cam* 1F **31**
Pentland Pl. *Cam* 4C **12**
Pentlands Clo. *Cam* 1E **21**
Pentlands Clo. *Cam* 1E **21**
Pepys Ter. *Imp* 5B **6**
Pepys Way. *Gir* 1D **11**
Percheron Clo. *Imp* 3C **6**
Perne Av. *Cam* 1B **30**
Perne Rd. *Cam* 1B **30**
Perowne St. *Cam* 4F **21**
Perry Ct. *Cam* 2F **19**
Perse Way. *Cam* .3C **12**
Peter Goodin Clo. *Mil* 4B **8**
Peterhouse M. *Cam* 4A **14**
Peterhouse Sports Ground. 3D **29**
Peterhouse Technology Pk.
 Cam 2E **31**
Peter Maitland Ct. *Cam* 5C **12**
Petersfield. Cam .3E **21**
 (off East Rd.)
Petersfield Mans. *Cam* 3E **21**
Pettit's Clo. *Ful* 3E **33**
Petty Cury. *Cam* 3C **20** (3D **3**)
Petworth St. *Cam* 2F **21**
Peverel Clo. *Cam* 1D **23**
Peverel Rd. *Cam* 1C **22**
Pierce La. *Ful* 2D **33**
Pikes Wlk. *Cam* 2D **21** (2F **3**)
Pine Ct. *Imp* 4B **6**
Pinehurst. *Cam* 4A **20** (5A **2**)
Pines, The. *Ful* 2D **33**
Pippin Dri. *Ches* .3B **14**
Plum Tree Clo. *Cam* 2B **12**
Pool Way. *Cam* 2B **22**
Poplar Rd. *His* 3A **6**
Porson Ct. *Cam* .3D **29**
Porson Rd. *Cam* .2D **29**
Portico Wlk. *Cam* 1D **13**
Portland Pl. *Cam* 2E **21** (2F **3**)
Portugal Pl. *Cam* 2C **20** (1D **3**)
Portugal St. *Cam* 2C **20** (1D **3**)
 (in two parts)
Post Office Ter. *Cam* 3D **21** (3E **3**)
Pound Hill. *Cam* 1B **20** (1B **2**)
Pretoria Rd. *Cam* 1E **21**
Primary Ct. *Cam* .4A **14**
Primrose Clo. *Cher H* 2F **31**
Primrose Cft. *Cam* 5C **12**
Primrose St. *Cam* 5C **12**
Prince Andrew Ct. Cam 5A **14**
 (off High St.)
Princes Ct. Cam .5D **21**
 (off Coronation St.)
Prince William Ct. *Cam* 5B **12**
Prior's Clo. *His* 2A **6**
Priory Rd. *Cam* 1F **21**
Priory Rd. *Horn* 5F **9**
Priory St. *Cam* 5B **12**
Prospect Row. *Cam* 3E **21** (3F **3**)
Pryor Clo. *Mil* 4C **8**
Purbeck Rd. *Cam* 2E **29**
Pye Ter. *Cam* 5F **13**

Q

Quainton Clo. *Cam* 1C **22**
Quayside. *Cam* 2C **20** (1C **2**)
Queen Edith's Way. *Cam* 3A **30**
Queens' College Sports Ground. 5E **19**
Queens' La. *Cam* 3C **20** (4C **2**)
Queen's Mdw. *Cam* 5E **23**
Queen's Rd. *Cam* 2B **20** (1B **2**)
Queensway. *Cam* 1D **29**
Queens Way. *Oak* 1C **4**
Quorum, The. *Cam* 2D **23**
Quy Rd. *Lode* 2F **17**

R

Rachel Clo. *Cam* 5D **15**
Rackham Clo. *Cam* 5B **12**
Radegund Rd. *Cam* 5A **22**
Railway St. *Cam* .5E **23**
Ramsden Sq. *Cam* 2F **13**
Rathmore Clo. *Cam* 1F **29**
Rathmore Rd. *Cam* 1F **29**
Ravensworth Gdns. *Cam* 5F **21**
Rawlyn Clo. *Cam* 1C **22**
Rawlyn Ct. *Cam* .1C **22**
Rawlyn Rd. *Cam* .1C **22**
Rayleigh Clo. *Cam* 2D **29**
Rayson Way. *Cam* 1C **22**
Recreation Clo. *Mil* 5C **8**
Rectory Ter. Cher H 1E **31**
 (off High St.)
Red Cross La. *Cam* 5A **30**
Redfern Clo. *Cam* 3D **13**
Redgate Rd. *Gir* .5D **5**
Redmond Ct. *Cam* 4A **22**
Redwood Lodge. *Cam* 4A **20**
Regatta Ct. *Cam* .5A **14**
Regency Sq. *Cam* 5F **21**
Regent St. *Cam* 3D **21** (4F **3**)
Regent Ter. *Cam* 3D **21** (4F **3**)
Reilly Way. *Cam* .4E **23**
Rexbury Ct. *Cam* 2F **21**
Ribston Way. *Cam* 3B **14**
Richmond Rd. *Cam* 5A **12**
Richmond Ter. *Cam* 1D **3**
Rickard Clo. *Cam* 1D **31**
Ridley Hall Rd. *Cam* 4B **20** (5B **2**)
Rivar Pl. *Cam* 3F **21**
River Ct. *Cam* 5A **14**
River La. *Cam* 1F **21**
Riverside. *Cam* 1F **21**
Riverside Ct. *Cam* 1D **21**
Robert Davies Ct. *Cam* 2A **14**
Robert Jennings Clo. *Cam* 3F **13**
Robert May Clo. *Cam* 5C **22**
Robinson Way. *Cam* 4F **29**
Rock Rd. *Cam* 1F **29**
Rodings, The. *Cam* 5D **15**
Roedeer Clo. *Cam* 5F **23**
Roland Clo. *Cam* 4D **13**
Roman Hill. *Bart* .3B **26**
Romsey M. *Cam* .4A **22**
Romsey Rd. *Cam* 4B **22**
Romsey Ter. *Cam* 4A **22**
Romsey Town. 4A **22**
Ronald Rolph Ct. *Cam* 5C **14**
Rose Cres. *Cam* 2C **20** (2D **3**)
Roseford Rd. *Cam* 3B **12**
Roselea. *Imp* 3B **6**
Rosemary La. *Cam* 4E **23**
ROSIE MATERNITY HOSPITAL. 4F **29**
Rosina Ct. *Cam* .4A **22**
Ross St. *Cam* 4A **22**
Rotherwick Way. *Cam* 4B **30**

Rothleigh Rd. *Cam* .2C **30**
Round Chu. St. *Cam* 2C **20** (1D **3**)
Rowans, The. *Mil* 4B **8**
Rowlinson Way. *Cam* 1A **22**
Roxburgh Rd. *Cam* 2D **13**
Royal Albert Almshouses. *Cam* 5E **21**
Royal Greenwich Observatory. 5F **11**
Rush Gro. *Cam* .1F **31**
Russell Ct. *Cam* 5D **21**
Russell St. *Cam* 5E **21**
Russet Ct. *Cam* 3B **14**
Rustat Rd. *Cam* 1F **29**
Rutherford Rd. *Cam* 3D **29**
Rutland Clo. *Cam* 3C **12**

S

Sable Clo. *Cam* 5F **23**
Sackville Clo. *Cam* 2D **13**
Sadlers Clo. *Cot* 2A **18**
Saffron Rd. *His* .3A **6**
St Albans Rd. *Cam* 3C **12**
St Andrews Glebe. *Cam* 5E **23**
St Andrew's Pk. *His* 1A **6**
St Andrew's Rd. *Cam* 1F **21**
St Andrew's St. *Cam* 3D **21** (3E **3**)
St Andrews Way. *Imp* 2D **7**
St Anthonys Wlk. *Cam* 5D **21**
St Audrey's Clo. *His* 2F **5**
St Barnabas Rd. *Cam* 4F **21**
St Bede's Cres. *Cam* 1D **31**
St Bede's Gdns. *Cam* 1D **31**
St Catharine's College Sports Ground. 5A **20**
St Catharines Hall. *Cot* 2B **18**
St Catharine's Rd. *Cam* 2C **12**
St Catharine's Sq. *Cam* 2C **12**
St Christopher's Av. *Cam* 5B **12**
St Clements Gdns. *Cam* 1D **3**
St Edward's Pas. *Cam* 3C **20** (3D **3**)
St Eligius Pl. *Cam* 4D **21**
St Eligius St. *Cam* 5D **21**
St George's Ct. *Cam* 2F **29**
St George's Way. *Imp* 3D **7**
St John's Innovation Cen. *Cam* 1B **14**
St John's La. *Horn* 4F **9**
St John's Pl. *Cam* 1B **20**
St John's Rd. *Cam* 1C **20** (1D **3**)
St John's Rd. *Cot* 2A **18**
St John's St. *Cam* 2C **20** (2D **3**)
St Kilda Av. *Cam* 2F **13**
St Lukes M. *Cam* 1C **20**
St Luke's St. *Cam* 1C **20**
St Margaret's Rd. *Gir* 3E **11**
St Margarets Sq. *Cam* 2A **30**
St Marks Ct. *Cam* 4B **20**
St Mary's Ct. *Cam* 2D **3**
St Mary's Pas. *Cam* 3C **20** (3D **3**)
St Mary's St. *Cam* 3C **20** (3D **3**)
St Matthew's Ct. *Cam* 2F **21**
St Matthew's Gdns. *Cam* 2F **21**
St Matthew's St. *Cam* 2F **21**
St Neots Rd. *Cax* 1A **18**
St Paul's Pl. *Cam* 4E **21**
(off St Paul's Wlk.)
St Paul's Rd. *Cam* 4E **21** (5F **3**)
St Paul's Wlk. *Cam* 4E **21** (5F **3**)
St Peter's Rd. *Cot* 2A **18**
St Peter's St. *Cam* 1B **20** (1B **2**)
St Peter's Ter. *Cam* 4C **20** (5D **3**)
St Philip's Rd. *Cam* 4A **22**
St Regis. *Cam* .5E **13**
St Stephen's Pl. *Cam* 5B **12**
St Thomas's Rd. *Cam* 1C **30**
St Thomas's Sq. *Cam* 1C **30**
St Tibb's Row. *Cam* 3D **21** (3E **3**)
St Vigor's Rd. *Ful* 3E **33**
St Vincent's Clo. *Gir* 1D **11**

Salisbury Pl. *Cam* 4C **28**
Salisbury Vs. *Cam* 5E **21**
Salmon La. *Cam* 2E **21** (2F **3**)
Sanders La. *Ful* 3F **33**
Sandwick Clo. *Cam* 1D **13**
Sandy La. *Cam* 5E **13**
Saxon Rd. *Cam* 1F **21**
Saxon St. *Cam* 4D **21** (5E **3**)
Scarsdale Clo. *Cam* 3A **14**
School Ct. *Cam* 4A **22**
School Hill. *His* .2A **6**
School La. *Bart* 3A **26**
School La. *Ful* .3E **33**
School La. *Imp* .3B **6**
Scotland Clo. *Cam* 4F **13**
Scotland Rd. *Cam* 5F **13**
Scotsdowne Rd. *Cam* 4C **28**
Scroope Ter. *Cam* 4C **20** (5E **3**)
Searle St. *Cam* 5C **12**
Sedgwick Mus. of Earth Sciences.
. . . . .3D **21** (4E **3**)
Sedgwick St. *Cam* 4A **22**
Sedley Taylor Rd. *Cam* 3E **29**
Sefton Clo. *Cam* 4C **28**
Selwyn Gdns. *Cam* 4A **20** (5A **2**)
Selwyn Rd. *Cam* 5A **20**
Senate Ho. Pas. *Cam* 3C **20** (3C **2**)
Severn Pl. *Cam* 2F **21**
Seymour Ct. *Cam* 4B **22**
Seymour St. *Cam* 4B **22**
Shaftesbury Rd. *Cam* 1E **29**
Shelford Bottom. 5C **31**
Shelford Rd. *Cam* 5C **28**
Shelford Rd. *Ful* 5F **31**
Shelly Garden. *Cam* 1B **20**
Shelly Row. *Cam* 1B **20**
Shenstone Ho. *Cam* 2F **21**
(off Staffordshire St.)
Shepherds Clo. *Fen D* 4E **15**
Shepherd's Clo. *Cam* 1F **31**
Sheppard Way. *Tev* 3A **24**
Sherbourne Clo. *Cam* 3A **14**
Sherbourne Ct. *Cam* 3A **14**
Sherlock Clo. *Cam* 5A **12**
Sherlock Ct. *Cam* 5A **12**
Sherlock Rd. *Cam* 5A **12**
Shirley Clo. *Mil* .4D **9**
Shirley Gro. *Cam* 4A **14**
Shirley Rd. *His* .3A **6**
Short Drove Way. *Tev* 5F **17**
Short St. *Cam* 2D **21** (2F **3**)
Sidgwick Av. *Cam* 4B **20** (5A **2**)
Sidney Farm Rd. *Cam* 1D **31**
Sidney St. *Cam* 2C **20** (2D **3**)
Signet Ct. *Cam* 1A **22**
Silverdale Av. *Cot* 2A **18**
Silverdale Clo. *Cot* 2A **18**
Silver St. *Cam* 4C **20** (5C **2**)
Silverwood Clo. *Cam* 2A **22**
Simons Ho. *Cam* 5B **12**
Sladwell Clo. *Gran* 4E **27**
Sleaford St. *Cam* 3F **21**
Somerset Clo. *Cam* 2C **12**
Somerset Rd. *His* 3F **5**
Somervell Ct. *Cam* 2D **13**
Southacre Clo. *Cam* 1D **29**
Southacre Dri. *Cam* 1D **29**
Southbrooke Clo. *Cam* 4C **28**
S. Green Rd. *Cam* 5B **20**
South Rd. *Imp* .5A **6**
Southside. *Cam* 4F **13**
Spalding Way. *Cam* 3C **30**
Speedwell Clo. *Cam* 1F **31**
Spens Av. *Cam* 4A **20**
Spinney, The. *Cam* 1B **30**
Spring Clo. *His* .2B **6**
Springfield Rd. *Cam* 5D **13**
Springfield Rd. *Imp* 5B **6**

Springfield Ter. *Cam* 5D **13**
Spurgeon's Clo. *Tev* 3A **24**
Square, The. *Horn* 5F **9**
Square, The. *Stow* .3F **17**
Stable Ind. Est. *Cam* 4C **14**
Stacey La. *Cam* 2F **19**
Staffordshire Gdns. Cam 2F **21**
                           (off Staffordshire St.)
Staffordshire St. *Cam* 2F **21**
Stanbury Clo. *Fen D* 3D **15**
Stanesfield Clo. *Cam* 1C **22**
Stanesfield Rd. *Cam* 1C **22**
Stanley Ct. *Cam* 1A **22**
Stanley Rd. *Cam* 1A **22**
Stansfield Gdns. *Ful* 2E **33**
Stansgate Av. *Cam* 4A **30**
Stanway Clo. *Cam* .2E **21**
Starling Clo. *Mil* 3C **8**
Station Rd. *Cam* 5E **21**
Station Rd. *Ful* 2F **33**
Station Rd. *His* 2A **6**
Station Rd. *Lode* 1D **17**
Station Yd. *Ful* 1F **33**
Sterndale Clo. *Gir* 5D **5**
Sterne Clo. *Cam* 1A **30**
Stevenson Ct. *Cam* 1F **21**
Stevenson Ho. *Cam* 4F **13**
Stirling Clo. *Cam* 4F **13**
Stockwell St. *Cam* .4A **22**
Stonebridge La. *Ful* 3F **33**
Stone St. *Cam* 3A **22**
Stone Ter. *Cam* 3A **22**
Storey's Way. *Cam* 5A **12**
Stott Gdns. *Cam* 3F **13**
Stourbridge Gro. *Cam* 3B **22**
Stow Cum Quy. 3F **17**
Stow Rd. *Stow* 4E **17**
Strangeways Rd. *Cam* 3C **30**
Stratfield Clo. *Cam* 4A **12**
Strathcarron Ct. *Cam* 2D **13**
Stretten Av. *Cam* 5C **12**
Stukeley Clo. *Cam* .4F **19**
Stulp Fld. Rd. *Gran* 3F **27**
Sturmer Clo. *Cam* .2C **12**
Sturton St. *Cam* 2F **21**
Suez Rd. *Cam* 5B **22**
                           (in two parts)
Summer Ct. *Cam* 1C **22**
Summerfield. *Cam* 4B **20** (5B **2**)
Sunflower St. *Cam* .2C **12**
Sunmead Wlk. *Cam* 1F **31**
Sunningdale Cvn. Pk. *Cam* 3C **14**
Sunnyside. *Cam* 2D **23**
Sunset Sq. *Cam* 2C **12**
Sun St. *Cam* 2F **21**
Sussex St. *Cam* 2D **21** (2E **3**)
Sutton Clo. *Mil* 3C **8**
Swann's Rd. *Cam* .5B **14**
Swann's Ter. *Cam* .4F **21**
Swifts Corner. *Ful* 2E **33**
Sycamore Clo. *Cam* 1C **30**
Sycamores, The. *Mil* 4B **8**
Sylvester Clo. *His* 3A **20**
Symonds Clo. *His* 2A **6**
Symonds La. *Gran* .3F **27**

T

Tabrum Clo. *Gran* 3E **27**
Talbot Ho. *Cam* 1E **31**
Tamarin Gdns. *Cam* 1F **31**
Taunton Clo. *Cam* .5C **22**
Tavistock Rd. *Cam* .3B **12**
Teasel Way. *Cam* 2F **31**
Tedder Way. *Cam* 3C **12**
Temple Ct. Cam 2D **13**
                          (off Hercules Clo.)

Templemore Clo. *Cam* 3A **30**
Tenby Clo. *Cam* 1F **31**
Tenison Av. *Cam* 4E **21**
Tenison Ct. *Cam* 4F **21**
Tenison Rd. *Cam* 5F **21**
Tennis Ct. Rd. *Cam* 3D **21** (4E **3**)
Tennis Ct. Ter. *Cam* 3D **21** (5D **3**)
Teversham. 3A **24**
Teversham Drift. *Cam* 5F **23**
Teversham Rd. *Ful* .1D **33**
Teynham St. *Cam* 5C **22**
Thetford Ter. *Cam* .1D **23**
Thirleby Clo. *Cam* 4C **12**
Thistle St. *Cam* 2C **12**
Thoday St. *Cam* 4A **22**
Thomas Rd. *Ful* 2C **32**
Thompson's La. *Cam* 2C **20** (1D **3**)
                           (in two parts)
Thorleye Rd. *Cam* .2C **22**
Thornton Clo. *Gir* 3F **11**
Thornton Ct. *Gir* 3E **11**
Thornton Rd. *Gir* 2E **11**
Thornton Way. *Gir* .3F **11**
Thorpe Way. *Cam* .5D **15**
Thrift's Wlk. *Cam* 5A **14**
Thulborn Clo. *Tev* 3A **24**
Tillyard Way. *Cam* .3C **30**
Tiptree Clo. *Cam* 5E **15**
Tiverton Way. *Cam* .5B **22**
Tom Amey Ct. *Cam* 4A **22**
Tomkins Mead Nature Reserve. 5C **8**
Topcliffe Way. *Cam* 4B **30**
Topham Way. *Cam* .3C **12**
Tourist Info. Cen. 3C **20** (3D **3**)
Town Clo. *Ful* 2E **33**
Townsend Clo. *Mil* 3C **8**
Trafalgar Rd. *Cam* .1D **21**
Trafalgar St. *Cam* 1D **21**
Tram Yd., The. Cam 3E **21**
                           (off Dover St.)
Tredegar Clo. *Cam* .3D **13**
Tredgold La. *Cam* 2E **21**
Trevone Pl. *Cam* 5B **22**
Tribune Ct. *Cam* 1D **13**
Trinity Hall Farm Ind. Est. *Cam* 2A **14**
Trinity La. *Cam* 3C **20** (3C **2**)
Trinity St. *Cam* 2C **20** (3D **3**)
Tripos Ct. *Cam* 1E **29**
Trumpington. 4C **28**
Trumpington Rd. *Cam* 3C **28** (5E **3**)
Trumpington St. *Cam* 3C **20** (4D **3**)
Trust Ct. *His* 4A **6**
Turpyn Ct. *Cam* 2D **13**
Tuscan Ct. *Cam* 4F **13**
Tweedale. *Cam* 2E **31**
Tweedsmuir Ct. *Cam* 2D **13**
Twickenham Ct. *Cam* 4E **13**

U

Union La. *Cam* 4E **13**
Union Rd. *Cam* 4D **21** (5F **3**)
University Mus. 3D **3**
Uphall Rd. *Cam* 3C **22**
Up. Gwydir St. *Cam* 3F **21**

V

Valerian Ct. *Cam* 2F **31**
Velos Wlk. Cam 5D **15**
                           (off Ann's Rd.)
Ventress Clo. *Cam* .2C **30**
Ventress Farm Ct. *Cam* 2D **31**
Verulam Way. *Cam* .2C **12**
Vicarage Dri. *Gran* .3F **27**
Vicarage Ter. *Cam* .3F **21**

Victoria Av. *Cam* 1D **21** (1F **3**)
Victoria Homes. *Cam* 5D **13**
Victoria Pk. *Cam* 5C **12**
Victoria Rd. *Cam* 1B **20**
Victoria St. *Cam* 3D **21** (3F **3**)
Villa Ct. *Cam* 1D **13**
Villa Pl. *Imp* 4B **6**
Villa Rd. *Imp* 4B **6**
Vinery Pk. *Cam* 4B **22**
Vinery Rd. *Cam* 4B **22**
Vinery Way. *Cam* 3B **22**
Vines, The. *Oak* 1B **4**
Violet Clo. *Cam* 2F **31**
Vision Pk. *His* 4A **6**

W

Wadloes Footpath. *Cam* 5D **15**
Wadloes Rd. *Cam* .5C **14**
Wagstaff Clo. *Cam* .2E **13**
Walker Ct. *Cam* 3D **13**
Walkling Way. *Mil* 4C **8**
Walnut Clo. *Mil* 4B **8**
Walnut Tree Av. *Cam* 1F **21**
Walnut Tree Way. *Cam* 2B **12**
Walpole Rd. *Cam* 2C **30**
Ward Rd. *Cam* 1C **30**
Warkworth St. *Cam* 3E **21** (3F **3**)
Warkworth Ter. *Cam* 3E **21** (3F **3**)
Warren Rd. *Cam* 4F **13**
Warwick Rd. *Cam* 4B **12**
Washpit Rd. *Gir* 1B **10**
Water La. *Cam* 4A **14**
Water La. *His* 3B **6**
Water La. *Oak* 1B **4**
Water St. *Cam* 5A **14**
Wavell Way. *Cam* 3D **13**
Weavers Fld. *Gir* 2D **11**
Wedgewood Dri. *Cher H* 1E **31**
Wellbrook Ct. *Gir* 2E **11**
Wellbrook Way. *Cam* 2E **11**
Wellington Ct. *Cam* 2F **21**
Wellington Pas. *Cam* 2F **21**
Wellington St. *Cam* 2E **21**
Welstead Rd. *Cam* .1F **31**
Wentworth Rd. *Cam* 5A **12**
Wenvoe Clo. *Cam* 1E **31**
Westberry Ct. *Cam* .4A **20**
Westbrook Cen. *Cam* 5D **13**
Westering, The. *Cam* 1D **23**
Westfield La. *Cam* .5B **12**
Westfield Rd. *Cam* .5B **12**
West Gdns. *Cam* 3B **20** (4A **2**)
Westgate. Cam 2D **31**
(off Carrick Clo.)
Weston Gro. *Ful* 2D **33**
West Rd. *Cam* 3B **20** (4A **2**)
West Rd. *His* 3A **6**
West Vw. *Cam* 5B **20**
Wetenhall Rd. *Cam* 4A **22**
Wheaton Ho. Cam .2F **21**
(off Staffordshire St.)
Wheeler St. *Cam* 3C **20** (3D **3**)
Wheelwright Way. *Stow* 3F **17**
Whipple Science Mus. 4D **3**
Whitefriars. *Cam* 4A **14**
Whitehill Clo. *Cam* .2C **22**
Whitehill Rd. *Cam* .1B **22**
Whitehouse La. *Cam* 4F **11**
Whitelock's. *Cam* 5B **28**

White Rose Wlk. *Cam* 2C **12**
Whitfield Clo. *Cam* .2E **13**
Whitgift Rd. *Tev* 4A **24**
Whitwell Way. *Cot* .2A **18**
Whyman's La. *Cam* .1B **20**
Whytford Clo. *Cam* .1F **21**
Widnall Clo. *Gran* 3E **27**
Wilberforce Rd. *Cam* 2A **20**
Wilbraham Rd. *Ful* .1F **33**
Wilderspin Clo. *Gir* .3E **11**
Wilding Wlk. *Cam* 4F **13**
Wiles Clo. *Cam* 2F **13**
Wilkin St. *Cam* 4F **21**
William Smith Clo. *Cam* 5F **21**
Willis Rd. *Cam* 3E **21**
Willowbank. *Cam* 1F **21**
Willow Cres. *Mil* 4C **8**
Willow Pl. *Cam* 2E **21** (2F **3**)
Willow Wlk. *Cam* 2E **21** (2F **3**)
Wilson Clo. *Cam* 3F **13**
Wilson Way. *Mil* 4C **8**
Wimpole Rd. *Bart* 4A **26**
Winchmore Dri. *Cam* 4B **28**
Windermere Clo. *Cam* 5F **23**
Winders La. *His* 1A **6**
Windlesham Clo. *Cam* 3D **13**
Windmill La. *Ful* 2D **33**
Windmill La. *His* 2A **6**
Windrush Cvn. Pk. *Cam* 1A **32**
Windsor Rd. *Cam* 4A **12**
Wingate Clo. *Cam* .4C **28**
Wingate Way. *Cam* .4C **28**
Winship Rd. *Mil* 5B **8**
Winstanley Ct. *Cam* 3A **22**
Woburn Clo. *Cam* 2D **13**
Wollaston Rd. *Cam* .3E **21**
Wolsey Way. *Cam* 5E **23**
Woodcock Clo. *Imp* .3C **6**
Woodhead Dri. *Cam* 3E **13**
Woodhouse Way. *Cam* 2F **13**
Woodlands Clo. *Gir* .5C **4**
Woodlands Pk. *Gir* .5C **4**
Woodlark Rd. *Cam* .4A **12**
Woodman Way. *Mil* .4C **8**
Woody Grn. *Gir* 1D **11**
Wootton Way. *Cam* .4F **19**
Wordsworth Gro. *Cam* 4B **20** (5A **2**)
World Conservation Monitoring Cen. 5F **11**
Worts Causeway. *Cam* 4B **30**
Wright's Clo. *Fen D* .3D **15**
Wrights Gro. *Ful* 3E **33**
Wulfstan Ct. *Cam* 3B **30**
Wulfstan Way. *Cam* 3B **30**
Wycliffe Rd. *Cam* 4B **22**
Wynborne Clo. *Cam* 4D **13**
Wynford Way. *Cam* .2D **13**

Y

Yarrow Rd. *Cam* 2F **31**
York St. *Cam* 2F **21**
York Ter. *Cam* 3F **21**
Youngman Av. *His* 1B **6**
Youngman Clo. *His* .1B **6**
Young St. *Cam* 2F **21**

Z

Zetland Wlk. *Cam* 5C **22**

INDEX TO COLLEGES

with their map square reference

Anglia Polytechnic University. 3E **21**

Cambridge Institute of Education. 1E **29**
Cambridge Regional College. 1E **13**
(King's Hedges Rd.)
Cambridge Regional College. 2E **21**
(Walnut Tree Av.)
Cambridge Regional College.
(Howes Close Country Cen.)
. . . . .3F **11**
(Whitehouse La.)
Cambridgeshire College of Agriculture & Horticulture.
. . . . .3C **8**
Cavendish Laboratory. 2E **19**
Christ's College. 2D **21** (2E **3**)
Churchill College. 1A **20**
Clare College. 3C **20** (3C **2**)
Clare College Playing Fields. 2E **19**
Clare Hall. 3A **20** (3A **2**)
Corpus Christi College. 4D **3**

Darwin College. 4C **20** (5C **2**)
Downing College. 4D **21** (5E **3**)

Edinburgh Building, The (Cambridge University Press)
. . . . .1E **29**
Emmanuel College. 3D **21** (3F **3**)

Fitzwilliam College. 5A **12**

Girton College. 3E **11**
Gonville & Caius College. 2C **2**

Harvey Court. 3B **20** (4B **2**)
Homerton College. .2F **29**
Hughes Hall. 4E **21**

Impington Village College. 3C **6**

Jesus College. 2D **21** (1F **3**)

King's College. 3C **20** (3C **2**)

Lady Mitchell Hall. 5A **2**
Leckhampton. 3A **20**
Lucy Cavendish College. 1B **20** (1A **2**)

Magdalene College. 1C **20** (1C **2**)

New Hall. 1B **20**

Old Schools. 3C **2**
Owlstone Croft (Queens' College) 5C **20**

Pembroke College. 3C **20** (4D **3**)
Pembroke College Sports Ground 5A **20**
Peterhouse. 4C **20** (5D **3**)

Queen's College. 3C **20** (4C **2**)
Queen's College Sports Ground. 5E **19**

Ridley Hall. 4B **20** (5B **2**)
Robinson College. 3A **20** (3A **2**)

St Catharine's College. 4C **2**
St Catharine's College Sports Ground. 5A **20**
St Edmund's College. 1B **20**
St John's College. 2C **20** (1C **2**)
St John's College Playing Fields. 2B **20** (1C **2**)
Selwyn College. 4B **20** (5A **2**)
Senate House. 3D **3**
Sidney Sussex College. 2D **21** (1E **3**)

Trinity College. 2C **20** (2C **2**)
Trinity Hall. 3C **20** (2C **2**)

University Cen. 4D **3**
University Department of Earth Sciences.
. . . . .5F **11**
University Observatories. 1F **19**
University of Cambridge Computer Laboratory.
. . . . .1F **19**
University of Cambridge School of
Veterinary Medicine 1D **19**
University Printing House. 2E **29**

Wesley House. 2D **21** (1E **3**)
Westcott House. 2D **21** (1E **3**)
Westminster College. 1B **20** (1B **2**)
Whittle Laboratory. .1F **19**
Wolfson College. 4A **20**
Wolfson Court (Girton College)
. . . . .2A **20** (1A **2**)